Where Was God
When Pagan Religions Began?

Where Was God When Pagan Religions Began?

by

Lester Sumrall

THOMAS NELSON PUBLISHERS
NASHVILLE

Unless otherwise indicated, all Scripture quotations are from the King James Version of the Bible.

Verses marked NKJB-NT in this publication are from *The New King James Bible-New Testament*. Copyright © 1979, Thomas Nelson, Inc., Publishers.

Verses marked RSV are from the Revised Standard Version of the Bible, copyrighted 1946, 1952, © 1971, 1973.

Verses marked TLB are taken from *The Living Bible* (Wheaton, Illinois: Tyndale House Publishers, 1971) and are used by permission.

Library of Congress Cataloging in Publication Data

Sumrall, Lester
  Where was God when pagan religions began?

  Includes bibliographical references
  1. Religion. 2. Paganism. I. Title.
BL 80,2,s 87   291   80-18829

ISBN 0-8407-5736-0

CONTENTS

INTRODUCTION

Critics insist that Christians should not try to change the beliefs of pagan people. They say that these people have believed as they do from the dawn of human history, so it is wrong for Christians to impose an alien belief system upon them. "Leave them alone," the critics say. "Let them enjoy the heritage of their culture."

This attitude arises from limited knowledge. It arises from historical misconceptions. It arises from a basic misconception of religion.

Notice the paradox: The critics of Christianity are willing to assist the people of pagan nations in all sorts of material ways. They feel a duty to share their knowledge of science and industry with them. Yet in matters of spiritual truth, they say that we should keep it to ourselves. They scream that we should leave the pagans alone.

The Christian cannot leave them alone. Anyone who loves God and has experienced the saving power of Jesus Christ cannot let other people die without an opportunity to know Christ. A Christian cannot look away from the need. He must face paganism, recognize it for what it is, and share the Good News of Christ with his pagan neighbors.

God told the prophet Ezekiel, "If you refuse to warn the wicked when I want you to tell them, You are under the penalty of death . . . they will die in their sins, but I will punish you. I will demand your blood for theirs" (Ezek. 3:18, TLB). God impressed this upon me, even before I read it in the Book of Ezekiel. It is a direct commandment from God. If we don't share the truth with other people, He will hold us accountable for their lives. He will find us guilty of losing their souls. Refusing to tell others about Jesus Christ is reckless spiritual homicide in the same way that killing another by doing foolish stunts with an automobile is reckless homicide. It condemns innocent people to death. When God revealed this to me, I was staggered by the enormous responsibility. I realized that He wanted me to spread the gospel around the world. I knew I had to do it in every way possible.

God went on to tell Ezekiel, "But if you warn him [the unbeliever] and he repents, he shall live and you have saved your own life too" (Ezek. 3:21, TLB). Isn't this a thrilling promise? You and I can help to save people who otherwise are doomed to die. We can't *guarantee* that they'll be saved; but we can give them what they need for salvation—the knowledge of Jesus Christ. Then the matter is in their hands. They can take Christ as their own personal Savior and live, or they can reject Him and perish. At least we have given them an opportunity to choose.

Hundreds of millions of people are living in the bondage of paganism. I have lived near them half of my life, in over one hundred nations of the world. They live in the chains of superstition, fear, and suspicion. The cause of most problems in non-Christian lands is religious, not social or political. These nations will not be free and strong until the individuals who live there are free and strong; only Christ can make them so (John 8:34–36).

Look at Hebrews 1:1–3. Here we read that God has appointed Jesus as the "heir of all things . . . upholding all things by the word of his power." In other words, God has appointed His Son, Jesus, to rule this world now and forever. No one else can rule with Him. No one else can save a person from his sins. No one else can offer a person eternal life; "He that entereth not by the door . . . but climbeth up some other way, the same is a thief and a robber" (John 10:1). So a person can be saved only through Jesus Christ.

Some callous Christians believe that God has ordained that the pagan nations should die without Christ. They feel that those who are born and raised in Christian lands are His "chosen people," and the rest, unfortunately, are not. This is not so. Scripture says that God is "not willing that any should perish, but that all should come to repentance" (2 Pet. 3:9). Theories about there being "chosen people" and "unchosen people" are just rationales for evangelistic laziness.

And pagan religions are no longer confined to foreign countries. During the past thirty years, we have seen a steady influx of pagan cults into the Western world. Many people have turned to Eastern religions, hoping to find a tranquil retreat from the problems of our society. So missionaries are not the only people who must be acquainted with the pagan religions. Any Christian may find that his neighbor, his boss, or even a member of his family is involved in a non-Christian religion. More than ever, Christians need to know what these pagan religions teach and learn how to respond to them.

An important question lies at the heart of such a study: "Where was God when these pagan religions began?" If the founders of these religions were earnestly searching for the truth, why didn't God reveal Himself to them? Was God's power not evident in their parts of the world? Were they deprived of the opportunity to know Him? And what about the millions of people who have adopted these pagan beliefs—why haven't they found God?

In this book, we will examine the origin of the greatest pagan religions in our world. We will study the environment in which the founders of these religions lived. We will see how these religions began to rule entire nations and empires. We will learn why they are so powerful today.

Also, we will see what God was doing in the lands where these religions were born. It will become obvious that God was trying to reveal Himself to these pagan peoples, as He did to the early Jews. But the pagan leaders chose to ignore Him; human stubbornness condemned them to live without God. And whether a pagan accepts God today is still a matter of human will, not of culture or tradition. The truth is just as true for a person who comes from a pagan background. It is less familiar, but just as true.

Lester Sumrall
South Bend, Indiana
Spring, 1980

Where Was God
When Pagan Religions Began?

1

GOD'S MASTER PLAN

The history of the world's religions is well-documented. You need not go far to find all the information you need about the pharaohs of Egypt, the kings of Babylon, the emperors of Rome, and the idolatrous religions they created. These ancient leaders left thousands of scrolls and inscriptions describing their beliefs, and any modern public library has several books about them.

As we study these pagan cults of the past, we find that they all emerged in a certain area of the world. All of them sprouted up among the populous nations of Southeast Asia and the Middle East—an area that runs like a wide, inverted crescent moon from the eastern end of the Mediterranean to the South Pacific. For some reason, this part of the world was a fertile seedbed for new religious ideas.

It was also the part of the world that had the best opportunities to see God at work.

Human history may be divided into several periods called *dispensations*, according to the way God has "poured out" His truth upon mankind in each successive age. Let's notice how God tried to communicate with the people in this part of the world under each dispensation.[1]

Innocence

First, God created the heavens and the earth. He made a place of paradise, called the Garden of Eden, where He placed Adam and Eve, the first man and woman He created. They loved God and served Him completely; this was the dispensation or era of *Innocence*.

Many theologians have speculated about what might have happened if Adam and Eve had remained in their innocent state. We will never know. But God promised them a happy, fruitful life if they obeyed Him, and we have every reason to believe that He intended for them to enjoy the pleasures of Eden. They had a relationship of complete harmony with God. They talked with God as we might chat with a neighbor over our backyard fence. God and man were intimate friends, and there was no such thing as a pagan religion.

Conscience

Then the man and woman decided to take charge of their lives. They disobeyed God in hopes of obtaining divine knowledge. So God condemned them to die for their sins, and He banished them from the garden. They entered a new relationship with God in which they found it more difficult to talk with Him and discern His will. They had to rely more on their own knowledge of good and evil. So this became the dispensation of *Conscience*.

Adam and Eve's son Cain killed his brother Abel in a fit of anger, so God drove him away from the family to start a new life of his own. Cain took a wife and had children; together they built a city and began to develop human civilization. Apparently, the first pagan religions appeared at this time. We have no formal records of when animism or other primitive religions began, but archaeologists have found many pagan idols that were made during this period. The Bible tells us that Cain's descendants were wicked people who fell into sexual perversion, murder, and other horrible sins.

Human Government

Conscience did not keep Adam and Eve and their descendants from sinning. In fact, they came to ignore God more and more, and to live as they pleased. To suppress this rampant sinfulness, God unleashed the great Flood, which destroyed all living things except a devout man named Noah, his family, and some animals they sheltered in their boat.

When the Flood subsided, Noah's sons went their separate ways to reestablish the great centers of civilization that had been destroyed. Their families pushed back the frontiers of the ancient wilderness, settling in different areas of Asia, Africa, and Europe.

17

God showed these people how to reorganize human society around local leaders who were responsible to Him. This was the age of the ancient city-states, in which a particular region was governed by the leaders of a city. God expected these leaders to honor and serve Him. Before long, however, they began to set themselves up as gods or blood relatives of gods and demanded that their subjects worship them.

God decided to separate them, knowing that a part of humanity might remain faithful to Him if the unfaithful were separated out. So as the leaders of the great city-states of Mesopotamia were building an enormous tower near the city of Babel, God confused their languages. They could no longer understand one another. Being already suspicious and jealous of their fellows, they quickly scattered into nations that became mutually hostile. Their pagan, human-centered religions destroyed the relationship they were supposed to have with God through their human governments.

Promise

From among these nations, God called a man named Abraham to go to the land of Canaan and establish a new nation that would be faithful to Him. He promised to make Abraham's descendants a very powerful nation. The noted theologian Louis Berkhof observes:

God appears unto Abraham again and again, repeating His promises, in order to engender faith in his

18

heart and to prompt its activity. The greatness of his faith was apparent in his believing against hope, in his trusting in the promise even when its fulfillment seemed a physical impossibility.[2]

Abraham, his father Terah, and their descendants had enough courage to answer God's call, even when He led them into strange foreign lands. Through all of their experiences, God shaped them into a nation that would represent Him in the ancient world. They became the torchlight of God's promise to the nations around them. God promised a home to Abraham's family (Gen. 15); He promised to "be their God" forever (Gen. 17:7,8). These promises governed their relationship with Him.

In the city of Jerusalem, God had appointed a priest and king named Melchizedek. This man met Abraham and blessed him by the authority of God Himself (Gen. 14:18–20). This proves that God did not leave mankind ignorant of the truth, even in those sinful times. He revealed Himself to men like Abraham and Melchizedek, who were seeking the true God.

When Abraham entered Egypt to escape a famine, God plagued the Egyptian pharaoh for taking Abraham's wife (Gen. 12:10–20). Three generations later, Abraham's descendant Joseph went to Egypt in slave chains and rose to a high rank in the Egyptian government. Later he arranged for his family to settle in the land of the pyramids. Four hundred years after that, God chose another of Abraham's descendants to lead His people out of

Egypt. Moses asked the pharaoh to "let my people go" so they could worship God. The pharaoh summoned his magicians to outperform the miracles of the Hebrew leader, but they couldn't. Their tricks seemed silly beside the holy power of God. Yet the pharaoh clung to his pagan beliefs.[3]

Notice that God did not coerce the pagan nations to follow Him. He revealed the truth to them and gave them an opportunity to respond; but if they rejected the truth, He chose some other way to accomplish His will. This shows God's patience and love for the people He created.

Law

God gave Moses a set of laws to govern His chosen nation. This began the dispensation of *Law*—a long period of time in which God's relations with man depended on how carefully man obeyed the laws that God prescribed.

God's Law began by saying, "Thou shalt have no other gods before me. Thou shalt not make unto thee any graven image. . ." (Ex. 20:3,4). Yet the pagan religions of Hinduism and Buddhism began during this dispensation. These religions claim that the world is literally teeming with gods—thousands of them—and that all these gods should be worshipped. Even God's own people began worshipping other gods. The kings of Israel bowed down to pagan idols and offered sacrifices to the false gods of their neighbors.

God raised up bold prophets to denounce this

20

apostasy. Through the prophets God said, "I am the LORD: that is my name: and my glory will I not give to another, neither my praise to graven images" (Is. 42:8). Yet the divided nation paid little attention to these messengers, and the kingdom was crushed by the armies of Assyria and Babylon.

I have visited several countries of the eastern Mediterranean and have brought back some of the pagan idols made at that time in history. These objects indicate what sort of perverse ideas the pagan worshippers had.

Some of the idols have a hole in the back of them where the spirit of the god is supposed to enter. Pagan worshippers believed that their gods would come to live in the idols they had made. Sometimes an idol has a small receptacle for burning incense. A priest would blow the incense smoke upon the worshippers' faces to show that the god's influence was coming upon them.

Many of the early pagan cults worshipped animals. The Egyptians worshipped cats, birds, and snakes; in fact, they preserved the bodies of these animals in special tombs because they considered them to be sacred. The Canaanites worshipped bulls; the Hindus worshipped cows. Today many tribes of Africa still name their children after sacred animals, hoping that they will enjoy the power of gods that supposedly live in those animals. The sociologist Emile Durkheim has observed:

> . . . Men regard the animals of the totemic species as kindly associates upon whom they can rely. They

call them to their aid and they come, to direct their
blows to the hunt and to give warning of whatever
dangers there may be. In return for this, men treat
[the animals] with regard and are never cruel to
them. . .[4]

This has been true of the animal cults from their
very beginning—under the dispensation of Law.
Men have tried to use magical powers to find security, pleasure, and contentment.

Let's take up the thread of history once again.
Judah fell to the Babylonians in 586 b.c. after dis-
obeying God for many generations. The ruler of
Babylon at that time was Nebuchadnezzar, who de-
signed Babylon's fabulous hanging gardens and its
intricate system of causeways and canals. The leaders of other nations knew that Nebuchadnezzar was
a wise, capable ruler, and many of them made al-
liances with him. When Nebuchadnezzar's armies
took Judah, he ordered them to bring the best of the
nation's leaders to Babylon, where they would
serve in his royal court.

One of these captives was Daniel, who predicted
that God would drive Nebuchadnezzar insane because he refused to worship Him. The prophecy
came true. The king went berserk and was driven
out of his own palace. He crawled around on all
fours, eating grass beside the oxen and sleeping in
open fields. His hair grew long and shaggy; his
fingernails became hard like claws as he rooted in
the dirt. His lunacy lasted for seven years. Then

God restored him to his right mind, and he returned to his throne. Nebuchadnezzar later said:

> . . . I blessed the most High, and I praised and honoured him that liveth for ever, whose dominion is an everlasting dominion, and his kingdom is from generation to generation (Dan. 4:34).

Although the witness of God-fearing people failed, and although a demonstration of God's power did not convince him,[5] God was able to change the king's mind by intervening in Nebuchadnezzar's own life. Obviously, God considered it very important to win this pagan king.

Soon another great culture arose—the Persian Empire. God used a Hebrew woman named Esther to persuade the Persian king not to kill the Jews in his domain (Esth. 8). Surely the king must have wondered where Esther got her courage and keen sense of justice. The answer was that she served the Lord God.

A later Persian king heard his Hebrew cupbearer ask for permission to return to his native land and granted the request. So Nehemiah returned to Jerusalem to rebuild the city and its walls so ravaged by wars with the superpowers of that day. When the walls were finished, Ezra the priest read aloud the written laws that God had given their ancestors through Moses (Neh. 8:1–3). God had a way of accomplishing His will—sometimes despite the pagan rulers, sometimes with their help.

Grace

When Jesus was born, a group of pagan astrologers came from the East to worship Him, following a star to the place where His family was staying. They did not know Old Testament prophecy, but they recognized that an earth-shaking event was taking place. The Bible says they came, not to honor Him as a king, but to worship Him (Matt. 2:11). No doubt they heard Mary tell how Jesus' birth had been announced to her by an angel and how the child had been conceived by the Holy Ghost. Surely they carried this news back to their native lands.

Indeed they had witnessed an important event. God had sent His own Son into the world to proclaim the message of His forgiveness and to die as a sacrifice for man's sin. Jesus' birth marked the beginning of a new dispensation of God's truth—the dispensation of *Grace*. In this phase of God's plan, we can have fellowship with Him again by accepting Jesus as our Savior and Lord.

Yet we should not overlook the way God deals with pagan religions during this new age, as evidenced in the ministry of Jesus Himself. Jesus frequently ministered to pagan individuals, and we can only imagine the impact this had upon their friends. For example, He healed the crippled servant of a Roman centurion (Luke 7:1–10, RSV). The centurion had heard of Jesus' powers, and he trusted Jesus' ability to heal his servant. In fact, he was so sure that Jesus could do it that he didn't even bring the slave to Jesus; he simply asked Jesus to "say the word, and let my servant be healed" (v. 7). Can you imagine that? Here was a Gentile man, a Roman soldier who literally had to worship the emperor to keep his job; yet he admitted to Jesus, ". . . I am not worthy to have you come under my roof" (v. 6), and he trusted Jesus to perform a long-distance miracle. Jesus was surprised. ". . . Not even in Israel have I found such faith," He said (v. 9). And He healed the servant.

It is hard to think that the centurion would have kept this news to himself. I think he would have told it over and over, perhaps to the emperor himself. Even if the centurion kept the story quiet, dozens of his pagan friends would have seen what happened. The truth was bound to get out.

Another day, Jesus was approached by a Canaanite woman from the region of Tyre and Sidon, an area where the Canaanites' pagan fertility cult was especially strong. They worshipped Baal, as well as other gods and goddesses. Yet this woman came to Jesus, pleading for Him to help her demon-possessed daughter.

At first, Jesus said, "I was sent only to the lost sheep of the house of Israel" (Matt. 15:24, RSV). Pagan people had no right to claim God's benefits, because they had never worshipped Him.

But the woman persisted: she acknowledged that Jesus was her "master" (Matt. 15:27, RSV), and she begged Him to exorcise the demons from her daughter.

"O woman," Jesus exclaimed, "great is your

faith! Be it done for you as you desire" (Matt. 15:28, RSV). Her daughter was delivered.

You see, Jesus cared about the needs of pagan people, and He praised them for the faith they had in Him. In fact, He longed for others who would lay aside their godless traditions and accept Him as their Lord.

Throughout the New Testament, we see God dealing with pagan people, trying to win them back to Him. Nowhere is this more obvious than on the day of Pentecost, when God poured out His Spirit on the Christians in Jerusalem.

Acts 2 tells us that Jesus' followers were waiting in Jerusalem, just as Jesus had instructed them, to receive the Holy Spirit who would guide and empower them for the ministry Christ had given them. They were destined to be there. God had a very special mission for them. Jewish people from many nations had gathered in the city to celebrate Pentecost. In the crowd were people from the various nations that had descended from each of Noah's sons. Think of it! Just as the human race met together beside Noah's ark to receive God's first covenant, they met together to receive the promise of His church. The descendants of Shem came from Europe; the descendants of Ham came from Africa; the descendants of Japheth came from Asia. Parthians, Medes, Egyptians, Romans, Syrians, Elamites—all of them were there! They saw the apostles filled with the Holy Spirit, and as the apostles filled with the Holy Spirit, and as the apostles spoke to them, they understood the gospel. At that moment, the church was born (Acts 2:1–21). The crowd listened intently to the message of the gospel, and about three thousand people accepted Christ (Acts 2:41). We can be sure that these people carried the gospel back to their pagan neighbors.

The Millennium

Scripture tells us there is one more dispensation to come, when Christ will return to earth and reign with His people for a thousand years (Rev. 20:4). During this time, He will bind Satan in a bottomless pit so that he cannot deceive men and women. It will be the first time in several millennia that God's great enemy will not be able to stir up rebellion against Him. It will be a time when pagan religions will disappear. Men and women will see Christ as He truly is, and they will live in perfect obedience to Him. It will be a foretaste of paradise.

But then Satan will be unloosed again, and he will marshal his forces of evil for his last battle with God (Rev. 20:7,8). Paganism will flare up more ferociously than we have ever known it, and it will consume many unsuspecting people. Everyone who deserts God to serve in the pagan ranks will be defeated, judged, and cast into the lake of fire (Rev. 20:13–15). Then God's eternal reign will begin.

Paganism and God's Plan

Do you see a pattern in all of this? I do. It becomes very obvious that God was revealing Himself

27

GOD'S PLAN OF THE AGES

←————— Eternity —————→

Innocence	Conscience	Human Government	Promise	Law	Grace	Millennium
(Gen. 2:16,17)	(Gen. 3:23)	(Gen. 8:20)	(Gen. 12:1)	(Ex. 19:8)	(John 1:7)	(Eph. 1:10)
The era prior to the Fall of man was a time of uninhibited communion between God and man.	After the Fall, humans had to rely primarily on their own knowledge of good and evil to govern their relationship with God.	After the Flood, human leaders emerged who were to govern the people in the fear of the Lord.	God established covenants, or promises, with Abraham and his descendants to govern their relationship with Him.	God gave Moses a set of laws to govern His people.	God sent His Son Jesus as the one through whom the gift of salvation would be made available to all people.	Christ will return to earth and rule for one thousand years.

to pagan peoples over and over again, in a variety of ways, seeking to bring them back to Him. Sometimes He succeeded, as on the day of Pentecost and on the sunny afternoon when Philip baptized the Ethiopian man (Acts 8:26–39). Many times pagans rejected Him. But God loved these unbelieving people so much that He attempted to reach them in any way possible.

In the present dispensation, God is still revealing Himself to the world. We Christians have a duty to share this revelation with our unbelieving neighbors. They must have an opportunity to hear the truth so they can decide whether to accept Christ.

2

THE CAUSE AND EFFECT OF PAGAN RELIGIONS

The most powerful force in the world today is not the atomic bomb. It is not the hydrogen bomb or the neutron bomb. The most powerful force in the world is religion.

We have seen this demonstrated quite dramatically in recent times. A fanatical cult leader has invited over four hundred people to commit suicide in the jungles of Guyana. A religious philosopher has seized control of Iran and established a so-called Islamic state. A kind, outgoing Pope from Poland traveled around the globe, and millions of people waited in stadiums and parks to hear what he had to say. Religion is more powerful than most people realize. It is the most exciting subject that you and I can discuss.

In the case of pagan religion, it can also be the most dangerous subject we can dicuss. The religions that deny God and defy His holy commands can destroy the soul of every person who follows them. They can rip apart the fabric of any nation that gives them shelter. They can throw the world into lawlessness and chaos.

We need to understand how pagan religions began

and how they affect the people who follow them. But first we need to define what we mean by a "pagan" religion.

Characteristics

Our English word *pagan* has a long history. We can trace it back to the early Latin word *pagus,* which meant "country." Later the word *paganus* emerged, meaning "country dweller." The Romans said that anyone who did not believe in their gods was a *paganus*—in other words, a country bumpkin who should know better. They probably would have called a Christian just another *paganus,* another "pagan." But when the Christians took control of the Empire, they started calling everyone else *pagani* (plural). And the name stuck. To this day, the word *pagan* means someone who is ignorant of God, someone who is a "country bumpkin" in terms of religion.

In the following chapters, I will show that every pagan person has ignored God, even though God's presence is obvious everywhere. God reveals Himself in a variety of ways to pagans, whether they live in the jungles of Africa or in the penthouses of Park Avenue. Pagans simply refuse to acknowledge Him.

Paganism is reflected in any action, belief, or attitude that operates as if God were not God. Let us examine the basic characteristics of pagan religion because I think they show how foolish paganism really is.

Paganism generally concerns itself with the

31

supernatural. A pagan claims to find meaning for his life beyond the real, sensible world. The pagan may follow a ritual of mystic chants and meditations, or repeat some regimen of illogical exercises, or sacrifice all of his possessions to a manmade idol—all in the name of his religion. Many pagans don't even realize they're worshipping. They think they're doing it for "kicks," for tradition, or for psychological security. In fact, they are closing out the real world—where God is trying to speak to them—hoping to find peace in some other imaginary world.

Paganism tends to involve *magic*—an outgrowth of its fondness for the supernatural. The pagan expects a miracle to solve his problems, and he thinks he can manipulate the supernatural forces in order to get the miracle he needs. He's fascinated by lucky charms, secret potions, and get-rich-quick schemes. He'll try first one, then another, trying to get the desired results.

Then there is *superstition,* also a common characteristic of paganism. While magic attempts to woo the supernatural forces of good, superstition attempts to repel the supernatural forces of evil. A superstitious person sees trouble lurking under every bedstead. He tries to avoid "unlucky" objects and "bad omens." Because he feels unprotected, he's afraid of doing anything that might expose him to evil. Thus the pagan is basically a fearful person.

Causes

How did these pagan religions begin? Anthropologists, sociologists, and philosophers have debated this question for generations. What prompted primitive people to begin worshipping idols? How did pagan religions survive their confrontations with Jews and Christians, people who worship the true God? Why do pagan religions continue to attract so many people if they are false?

The answers to these questions are no deep secret. The apostle Paul explained it to the Christians at Rome nearly two thousand years ago. Here's what he said about pagans:

> Since the creation of the world [God's] invisible attributes are clearly seen, being understood by the things that are made, even His eternal power and Godhead, so that they are without excuse, because, although they knew God, they did not glorify Him as God, nor were thankful, but became futile in their thoughts, and their foolish hearts were darkened. Professing to be wise, they became fools, and changed the glory of the incorruptible God into an image made like corruptible man, birds, four-footed beasts, and creeping things.

> Therefore God also gave them up to uncleanness, in the lusts of their hearts, to dishonor their bodies among themselves, who exchanged the truth of God for a lie, and worshiped and served the creature

rather than the Creator, who is blessed forever . . .
(Rom. 1:20–25 NKJB-NT).

So in the strictest sense, it is wrong to call these
people pagans. Though they act as if they are ignorant of God, they are well aware of Him; they simply
reject Him in favor of their own pet "gods." They
turn God's truth into lies. They distort reality into
whatever image they prefer.

Paganism begins when people worship God's
creatures instead of God Himself, the Creator. They
know that animals, idols, and mythical characters
will not demand as much from them as God demands. He is a holy God, and He demands that a
person's entire life be yielded to Him. Pagans resist
that. They would rather worship something that allows them to feel "religious" without making a full
surrender of their lives.

Paganism begins when people try to create substi-
tutes for the holiness of God. When sin infects a
person's life, that person will tremble in fear of God.
He needs God; he needs the firm anchor of God's
fellowship. Yet he knows that a sinner can have no
fellowship with a holy God. So he tries to create a
makeshift god—a not-so-holy god, one that he can
be comfortable with. This motive underlies all
idolatry, all heresy, and all kinds of watered-down
Christianity. It is a pagan motive.

Finally, paganism begins when a person is willing
to be deceived. Whenever someone allows himself
to entertain ungodly ideas just because they are en-

ticing, pleasurable, or ego-satisfying, he can be lured away from God. Paul told Timothy that the people who fall into paganism are those who are ". . . giving heed to seducing spirits, and doctrines of devils; speaking lies in hyprocrisy; having their conscience seared with a hot iron" (1 Tim. 4:1,2).

This is a matter of choice. Just as a person can permit his body to be seduced into an illicit sexual relationship, he can permit his soul to be seduced into an illicit spiritual relationship. Every person is free to decide whether to follow God or to follow a deception. Pagans have chosen to be deceived.

So these four elements frame the beginning of paganism—falsehood, creatureliness, sinfulness, and deception. These four ingredients compose the soil where pagan ideas take root and grow.

Effects

But what of the effects of paganism? What sorts of things happen in the life of a person who forsakes God for pagan ideals? The Bible tells us so much about this, and everyday life confirms what it says.

Scripture declares that in the last days more people will turn to heathen religions, idolatry, and superstition (1 Tim. 4:1); it says that these things destroy a person's vital contact with God (Rom. 11:22). A pagan is "cut off" from the God of life.

Paganism depraves a person's morals; godlessness and moral corruption go hand-in-hand. When one turns his back on God, he snaps the anchor chain that would hold him steady in the storm of moral decision. He casts himself adrift on an ocean of ethical uncertainty. Very soon, he slips into habits that bring anguish to his own life and the lives of everyone around him. God's Word says that if a person

> . . . hath lifted up his eyes to the idols, hath committed abomination, . . . shall he then live? he shall not live: he hath done all these abominations; he shall surely die; his blood shall be upon him (Ezek. 18:12, 13).

A person who turns from God slips into an attitude of fear and superstition. He feels intimidated by all the evil forces—both real and imagined—that surround him. He is afraid to begin any great endeavor; he is cautious about committing himself to anything that requires personal discipline. Why? Because he feels himself at the mercy of a myriad of supernatural forces, and he cannot anticipate how he should act. This is why few tremendous thinkers have come from pagan backgrounds. Their minds are bound by Satan's fears and doubts.

Because the pagan is fearful and insecure, he creates elaborate institutions to give him a sense of security. This is especially evident in pagan religions, which often have a complex hierarchy of spiritual leaders with impressive titles and neatly-drawn lines of authority. If someone is designated to answer his questions, indulge his mistakes, and tell him what to do with his life, the pagan feels secure. He thinks the institution takes the place of God.

Another result of paganism, but one that pagans seldom realize, is the worship of demons. Most people who reject God to adopt their own free-wheeling life-styles think they're worshipping no one, but they are indeed. They simply have shifted their priorities. And whatever they devote their lives to—whether it's making money, building a healthy body, climbing the ladder of social prestige, or whatever—that object of devotion is their false god. It is their idol. And the Bible says that anything we give to a false god is given to demons, or devils, whether we realize it or not.

> . . . The things which the Gentiles sacrifice, they sacrifice to devils, and not to God: . . . Ye cannot drink the cup of the Lord and the cup of devils: ye cannot be partakers of the Lord's table, and of the table of devils. Do we provoke the Lord to jealousy? are we stronger than He? (1 Cor. 10:20–22).

In my earlier book on demons, I explained how a person can leave himself vulnerable to demon possession.[1] I pointed out that Satan has many "subtle snares" to seize control of someone's life. Here is another one—the snare of wayward religion. A person who abandons the one true God to experiment with the false gods of this world is flirting with disaster. Such a person is unwittingly worshipping demons—the ungodly spirits that stand ready to rush in and fill the void in a soul without God. This is the most destructive result of drifting into paganism.

Signs of the Times

All around us, we see the effects of rampant paganism in America. The American people have an uncanny curiosity about foreign religions, and since World War II we have seen an incredible influx of non-Christian religions into this country. Along with foreign TV sets, foreign cars, and foreign oil we have imported foreign religion. Thousands of young people on our college campuses have become disciples of Buddhism, Hinduism, and other Eastern religions. Housewives scoop up books about mysticism and reincarnation as they pass through the check-out lanes of supermarkets. Business executives try the meditation techniques of Himalayan gurus, hoping to find peace of mind. If you tell any of these people they are practicing a pagan religion, they'll laugh at you. Yet that's exactly what they're doing.

But paganism is seeping into America in many other ways more subtle than the Hare Krishna beggars or Sun Myung Moon's flower vendors. We Americans are adopting *pagan attitudes* toward every facet of life. We are ignoring God's authority over our families, our jobs, our social contacts, and even our private thoughts. We are trying to ease God out the back door. Without realizing it, we are inviting paganism in the front door.

For example, many Americans take the Lord's Day for granted. It has become about the most popular business day of the entire week. Often, more money is spent in shopping malls and at sporting events on Sunday than on any other day. Yet God says, "Remember the sabbath day, to keep it holy" (Ex. 20:8). Modern Americans are glad to observe Sunday as a day of rest, but not as a day of worship. They have set it apart, not for God, but for personal business and pleasure. This is a pagan attitude.

Again, God says, "Honor thy father and thy mother: that thy days may be long upon the land which the Lord thy God giveth thee" (Ex. 20:12). This is a vital part of God's covenant with the human family, a command to respect our earthly parents in deference to our heavenly Father. Yet in this day of "children's rights," the trend is just the opposite. Parents are scorned; children are honored. Maturity is mocked; childishness is glorified. These are pagan attitudes.

Review the Ten Commandments very carefully and ask yourself, "Is America obeying God?" The answer is clearly evident in the way we Americans conduct ourselves. The effects of a godly life-style are easy to identify, and so are the effects of a pagan life-style. Our nation is rushing headlong into paganism, and I tremble to think of the consequences.

I said at the beginning of this chapter that religion is the most powerful force in the world. I firmly believe that. When people take up pagan religions, they weaken their nations and allow Satan to take control. The nations of our world that are in the throes of revolution, violence, and death got there by allowing paganism to weaken them.

In the following chapters we will see what paganism has done to nations where ungodly religions have dominated the scene for several generations. We will see the consequences of the ignorance and superstition that is the natural environment caused by pagan religions. We will see that the people of these nations are starving and dying of common diseases, because they don't know how to do otherwise, or because they are afraid to do otherwise. If you were to imagine that a cow was a god, you would not eat the cow; you would go hungry. If you believed that a flea or a tick was the reincarnation of one of your dead ancestors, you would not kill it; you would suffer from the diseases it might carry. This is exactly the predicament of many people who live in paganism today.

Thank God, our nation has not degenerated to these extremes. But the seeds of destruction are growing, and the tendrils of paganism are reaching into every nook and cranny of the American way of life. The causes of paganism are here; the effects of paganism are here.

Is God still here?

3
ANIMISM:
Religion of Fear

Animism is probably the oldest form of paganism. We have no written records of its beginnings, and no one person is remembered as its founder. Yet animism prevails in nearly every part of the world. It is truly an international form of paganism.

The religion of animism acts like a virus: It attaches itself to other religions and infects them with its ideas. Some of the most powerful religions of the ancient world, such as the emperor worship of Rome, grew sick and died through the weakening influence of animism.

A Religion of Spirits

What is animism? Basically, animism is a religion of spirits. It teaches that all of the physical elements of the world are inhabited by spirits—the spirits of dead ancestors or spirits that have never been embodied as human beings. The people who accept animism believe they are surrounded by spirits that they should worship and try to please. The noted anthropologists Ralph Beals and Harry Hoijer tell us that animism has such a vague understanding of the spirit world that virtually everything has some religious importance. They define animism as

> . . . a belief or set of beliefs in supernatural beings . . . who may dwell in natural phenomena such as trees, pools, and mountains, in artifacts, such as weapons, houses, or boats, or who may simply exist invisibly in some portion or all of the universe.

> The variety and types of supernatural beings in which [animists] believe is so great as almost to defy either enumeration or classification.[1]

Most of the primitive tribes of the world are steeped in a long tradition of animism. They think spirits inhabit everything that they see or touch, and they feel a duty to worship all of the spirits—even the evil spirits. In this respect, they practice a form of *pantheism* (the worship of all gods).

Animism attempts to control spirits to get specific, desired results. This is why witchcraft thrives among people who believe in animism. Animists think that the witch doctor's magic potions and chants will persuade the spirits to do what is wanted. The witch doctors say they can cause spirits to leave one person's body and enter another. They work themselves into a frenzy, dancing and shouting and jabbering all kinds of magic formulas. All of this is supposed to marshal the spirits at the worshipper's beck and call.

A central part of animism is the *fetish*. This is any object considered especially holy and able to charm good spirits into helping the person who wears it. I brought back a fetish made of a serpent's tail from one of my trips to the Philippines. The people who use this type of fetish believe that a very strong spirit lives within a serpent, so they use the serpent's tail for their "good luck charm." They hollow out the tail, fill it with herbs and incense, then light the mixture. The smoke is supposed to have tremendous powers to grant the wishes of whoever carries the fetish.

While I was in the Philippines I opened six churches among the tribes of head-hunters who lived near Manila. At the center of one tribal village, I found a dead tree that was the focus of the tribe's worship. It was the most wicked-looking tree I've ever seen. It was crooked, gnarled, leafless (in the midst of the jungle's lush vegetation), and greasy from being rubbed daily by the hands of all the villagers. They tied their prayer ribbons to it. At the base of the trunk was a little altar where they burned incense and offered sacrifices of rice and wine. Every day the people prayed to the spirit of the tree. You couldn't convince them that the tree was not alive or that there wasn't a tree spirit who did things for them—you couldn't, that is, until they came to know the Lord Jesus Christ!

Animism shows that it's not enough for a person to be "spiritual." An animist can be very mindful of the spirit world; he can take his mind off personal gain and devote himself to the supernatural. But unless he devotes himself to God, he is lost. A spiritual religion is not enough. We need a religion filled with God's Holy Spirit.

A Religion of Fear

Animism causes people to live in a state of fear. In primitive societies, the people spend most of their time and effort seeking relief from vengeful spirits that they believe inhabit the trees, rocks, and mountains around them. These people are afraid of all the natural forces. They are afraid of wind, rain, fire, and earthquakes. They think the evil spirits of these elements are trying to harm them.

The people who believe in animism also fear one another, because they never know when someone might use spiritual powers to take advantage of them. It is common for a native to ask his witch doctor to put a curse on his enemies. He may ask the spirit of a boulder to fall on a rival as he walks along the jungle path. Or he may try to afflict the spirit of someone he resented after that person is dead.

> . . . One man requested his family to cut his corpse into two pieces to be buried in separate graves, for fear that the local sorcerer, who was his enemy, would bring him to life as a wretched slave. The Haitian government . . . sanctioned the belief by recently passing a law against the supposed practice [of making zombies].[2]

We cannot imagine the sheer terror that the followers of animism must feel. They think everyone—everything—is out to get them. They seem to be living in a hostile world, where they must be careful to appease every spirit or run the risk of unspeakable punishment. They have a religion of fear.

A Dogma

We Westerners tend to think that the religions of primitive tribes are nothing more than emotion or tradition. We suppose that the savages know they have some sort of "pretend" religion and that they will quickly abandon it for the truth as soon as they hear it. That is a myth.

Animism is more than an emotion or a tradition. It is a dogma. These people have been taught to believe from earliest childhood that they are surrounded by spirits who need to be satisfied. Tribal chiefs teach this to their followers. Witch doctors, the most highly educated people of the tribe, teach it to their apprentices. It is a doctrine deeply ingrained in the minds of the people who live in animism. It is accepted as the honest truth and embellished with interpretations and applications to suit every problem that might arise. Animists feel confident that their religion is the only true religion and that everything else is folly.

God's Response

As we've seen, God's first command in the Ten Commandments was, "Thou shalt have no other gods before me" (Ex. 20:3). Generations later, He said, "There shall no strange god be in thee; neither shalt thou worship any strange god'' (Ps. 81:9). Yet the people of Israel succumbed to paganism again and again, even accepting the primitive ideas of animism. God told Jeremiah, "Hast thou seen that which backsliding Israel hath done? she is gone up upon every high mountain and under every green tree, and there hath played the harlot" (Jer. 3:6). One day Ezekiel found twenty-five men on the porch of the temple in Jerusalem, bowing to worship the sun. God said to him, "Hast thou seen this, O son of man? Is it a light thing to the house of Judah that they commit the abominations which they commit here?" (Ezek. 8:17).

Make no mistake: God hates animism. He hates it because it is nothing more than Satan worship. An animist is not worshipping an ideology, or a tradition, or the spirit of a tree; he is worshipping Satan, who tries to trick everyone into worshipping him instead of God (cf. Is. 14:12–15). That is why Satan was thrown out of heaven; he wanted to be worshipped just as God is.

The power of God is always stronger than the power of Satan. The truth of the gospel can wipe out the lies of animism if we have enough courage to declare the truth. Acts 17:30,31 says, "And the times of this ignorance [i.e., the ancient past when paganism began] God winked at: but now commandeth all men every where to repent: because . . . he will judge the world in righteousness by that man whom he hath ordained." We have never more urgently needed to warn the people blinded by animism to repent and give their lives to God.

Earlier, I mentioned visiting a village in the Philippines where head-hunters worshipped the spirit of an old, gnarled tree. I held a meeting in that village one evening. I told the people about the Lord Jesus Christ and His great love for them. As I was speaking, the head priestess who ruled them through the tree began to make a strange roaring noise. It was eerie. She stood at the edge of our circle and growled louder and louder, trying to distract the people. I didn't know who she was, since I was only a visitor. But I pointed my finger at her and said, "Upon the authority of the Word of God,[3] I command you to stop. I command you to be speechless. I command you never to disturb a worship service again." She fell silent. The villagers later told me that she was speechless for about forty-eight hours, and when she regained her voice she said she never wanted to go to a service like that again.

I met a man, the mayor of a town in Indonesia, who once had been a witch doctor. He had challenged a woman missionary to a test of power. He'd said, "I am stronger than you are. If your God is so powerful, let him match his powers against mine."

So the two agreed to meet before the witch doctor's whole village. They secluded themselves for two days to prepare for the confrontation.

When they met at the hut where they were supposed to test their powers, the timid little missionary lady didn't know what to do first. So she said, "You do something."

The witch doctor stretched himself out on the dirt floor and stiffened his body. He asked his pagan spirits to give him the power of levitation. Sure enough, he just floated up into the air about knee high and hovered there, effortlessly.

The missionary lady started to pray. "Listen, God," she said. "You know I can't float in the air. So what am I going to do? Leave town, defeated?"

The Lord seemed to say, "No, get him down."

"But how can I get him down?" she prayed.

"Put your foot on him."

So the missionary lady lifted her skirt and planted her foot on the witch doctor's chest. She pushed his body back to the floor. And then she said, "Come out of him. Come out of him now. In the name of Jesus, I command you to come out."

The witch doctor laid there for a few minutes. Then he opened his eyes and said, "Where am I?" The evil spirits had left him.

In that same meeting, the missionary led him to accept Jesus Christ as his Savior; she laid hands on him and asked God to give him the power of the Holy Spirit. Together they started a new village that they called the Town of Refuge. When I visited it, over five hundred adults lived there. They had come to the Town of Refuge for protection from the people all around them who practiced witchcraft. The witch doctor became the mayor of the city—all because God's power is greater than the devil's power.

The people who are controlled by animism need the love of God. Scripture says:

> In this our love has been made perfect, that we may have boldness in the day of judgment; because as He is, so are we in this world. There is no fear in love; but perfect love casts out fear, because fear involves torment. But he who fears has not been made perfect in love (1 John 4:17,18, NKJV-NT).

When a person receives the fullness of God, he doesn't fear anyone or anything. The people who believe in animism live in terrible fear; they need to know the true God, who is loving and merciful. They need to know that their heavenly Father cares for them, even when the disasters of fire, flood, and earthquake devastate their lives.

Pray that God will send more of His laborers into the vineyard of missionary work to set these people free.

4
EGYPTIAN RELIGION:
A Pattern for America?

Most of us think of Egypt as a Muslim country, the most powerful Arab nation in the Middle East. Situated on the northeast shoulder of Africa, Egypt has a population of over thirty-two million. It is one of the most progressive nations in its part of the world, and other nations are anxious to see what will come out of Egypt's new peace treaty with Israel. Egypt is a Muslim country; Israel is a Jewish country. Yet they have resolved to live at peace with one another.

Sprawling, bustling, trying to move forward—this is the Egypt we know from the newspaper headlines. But Egypt is also a very ancient country. Its first united government was formed about 3200 B.C., more than one thousand years before the time of Abraham. Egypt became one of the greatest powers of antiquity, controlling much of the Mediterranean area. The nations of old looked to Egypt for commodities like cotton, grain, and gold. They also absorbed new ideas from Egypt; after all, this was the elite civilization that produced the marvelous pyramids and other superb feats of architectural design. The ancients respected Egypt for her knowledge.

Egypt often controlled Canaan as one of its "buffer states"—a frontier nation to insulate the Egyptians from their enemies. The Egyptians feared the Babylonians and Assyrians who lived to the east, as well as the Hittites and the "Sea People" who lived to the north. So they tried to keep Canaan under the thumb of Egypt, as a matter of national security. Egypt was an important factor in the ancient balance of power, just as it is today.

God had a vital interest in Egypt—not so much because it was a powerful nation, although it certainly was powerful—but because of the millions of people who lived there under the bondage of paganism.

At a very early stage, God arranged to bring the message of His covenant to the Egyptians. God told Abraham, ". . . In thee shall all families of the earth be blessed" (Gen. 12:3), and Egypt received that blessing eventually. One of Abraham's sons, Ishmael, was born of an Egyptian woman, Hagar (Gen. 16:1). The historian Josephus says that Ishmael married an Egyptian.[1] Ishmael's descendants went to live along the border of Egypt (Gen. 25:18), and they traded with the Egyptians (Gen. 37:25; 39:1). Through them, the Egyptians had an opportunity to hear about God's new covenant with mankind. But the Egyptians paid no heed.

Egypt's Gods

During the dispensation of Promise, while God was making new promises and commitments to mankind, the Egyptians were wandering into paganism. They began worshipping false gods. Dr. William Smith says:

> The basis of the religion was Nigritian [i.e., African] fetishism, the lowest kind of nature worship, differing in different parts of the country, and hence obviously indigenous.[2]

The sun god Re was the chief pagan god that the Egyptians worshipped, praying to the sun as it rose each morning. Egypt had an agricultural economy, so the Egyptians depended on the sun to grow their crops and give them prosperity. They naturally assumed that the sun was a god, and the most powerful god at that.

Each city had its own favorite god who was supposed to be the spirit of that city. When one city defeated another in battle, the victors said it was because their god was stronger than the god of the city they'd defeated. So when the city of Thebes emerged as the capital of the united kingdom of Egypt, the people thought that Amun, the god of Thebes, was the most powerful god. That meant he was the same as Re. So they called him "Amun-Re," and made him the chief deity of the nation.

The Egyptians also worshipped animals, because they thought the spirits of gods lived in animals. They built sacred ponds for crocodiles. They maintained lavish temples for cats. They embalmed the bodies of falcons, monkeys, and other animals, giving them more lavish treatment than common laborers received.

They worshipped gods who were part human, part animal. We see evidence of this in ruins like the Sphinx, which has the head of a man and the body of a lion. Another statue has the head of a cat and the body of a woman, and another has the head of a falcon and the body of a man.

The Egyptians thought that even a beetle was sacred. I have a double handful of *scarabs*—little stone images of beetles that the Egyptians used as fetishes. Beetles! I think it is remarkable that Satan could so debase the intelligence of people—people who could engineer the construction of the pyramids—so that they worshipped bugs that crawl on the ground. This shows how paganism can destroy a nation.

God's Messengers

We have already seen that God led Abraham into Egypt; we have seen that Abraham's descendants through Ishmael settled beside the Egyptians. Each of these contacts warned the Egyptians to turn from their pagan ways and serve the true God. When they paid no attention, God kept on trying to reach them.

He arranged for Jacob to spend his last years in Egypt. Now who was better qualified than Jacob to tell the Egyptians the truth about God? He had seen a vision of angels descending from the throne of God

(Gen. 28:12–16). He wrestled with an angel to obtain God's blessing (Gen. 32:24–30). He became the heir of God's promise to Abraham. The Bible says that when Jacob met the pharaoh of Egypt, he gave the pharaoh God's blessing (Gen. 47:10); he did not keep his faith a secret.

God sent Jacob's son Joseph into Egypt and gave him the ability to interpret dreams, which brought him to the pharaoh's attention. Joseph plainly told the pharaoh,

> . . . What God is about to do he sheweth unto Pharaoh. . . . It is because the thing is established by God, and God will shortly bring it to pass (Gen. 41:28–32).

The pharaoh was so impressed by Joseph's powers that he gave him authority over all the wealth of his kingdom. He said, "Forasmuch as God hath shewed thee all this, there is none so discreet and wise as thou art" (Gen. 41:39). He told his advisors that Joseph was a man "in whom the Spirit of God is" (Gen. 41:38).

Here were men of God who talked to the leaders of the then-most-powerful nation in the world. They told the pharaohs about the true, living God. This pagan nation deserved to hear about God, and God gave them many contacts with the truth.

We find the same situation in Soviet Russia today. The Word of God is leaking into Russia, despite all the efforts of Communist officials to keep it out. Tourists carry Bibles and tracts across the border;

shortwave radio programs give the Bible passages slowly, word by word, so that Russian listeners can write them down; ministers slip through the Iron Curtain to visit their relatives and preach the gospel in secret meetings. No one can stop the Word of God from reaching its target. So it was in the days of ancient Egypt. God was speaking to the pharaohs, but they chose to keep their pagan gods instead of submitting themselves to the life of holiness that God demands of His people.

When Moses entered Egypt to lead his people out of slavery, he found that the new pharaoh had sold out to paganism. The pharaoh said, "Who is the Lord, that I should obey his voice to let Israel go?" (Ex. 5:2). Just four hundred years earlier, the Egyptians were singing the praises of Joseph and his all-knowing God. But now the nation had a pharaoh who "knew not Joseph" (Ex. 1:8) nor the God of Joseph. Therefore, he fought against God. And he lost.

Confronted by God's messenger, the pharaoh reacted in a typically pagan way. He turned to magic.

> Then Pharaoh also called the wise men and the sorcerers: . . . the magicians of Egypt, [who] also did in like manner with their enchantments (Ex. 7:11).

But the pagan magicians were no match for the power of God. Moses and Aaron called upon God and received more stunning miracles than the sorcerers ever could have imagined. God struck Egypt with ten great plagues, each more terrible than the one before, until the pharaoh agreed to let God's people go.[3] In the process, the pharaoh lost his firstborn son. When he changed his mind at the last minute and tried to bring the Hebrews back, he lost his army (Ex. 14:17,18,28).

When the Egyptians saw the results of the God who had power to open up the Red Sea and to slay people in their homes with an angel of death, they should have said, "We're going to serve that God." But they didn't. They kept on worshipping their pagan deities. The pharaohs gradualy lost their power and Egypt was overrun by the Greeks and Romans, who plundered the nation's gold and destroyed its magnificent buildings. The spiritual decay of Egypt ended in utter social and political collapse.

God's Love Continues

When the kingdom of Judah fell to the Assyrians in 586 B.C., many Jews fled to Egypt to avoid being captured. They established communities along the Nile River at places like Elephantine Island, where they built a small temple and tried to continue their sacrificial system. While the scribes of Elephantine copied the Old Testament Scriptures, many other able-bodied men of the community served in Egypt's army. Again, God gave the Egyptians an opportunity to see His covenant in action.

When Jesus was born, Mary and Joseph took him

to Egypt to escape Herod's soldiers (Matt. 2:13). Later, they returned to Judea. This fulfilled a long-standing prophecy that the Messiah would come up from Egypt (Num. 24:8; Hos. 11:1). So God kept on reaching out to Egypt, even in New Testament times.

Egyptian Jews were in Jerusalem on the Day of Pentecost, and they heard the apostles speaking in other languages (Acts 2:10). Very likely, some of them were converted to Christ (cf. Acts 2:41).

Soon afterward, the apostle Philip met a government official from "Ethiopia" riding in his chariot along the Gaza road, reading the Book of Isaiah (Acts 8:26–40). Bible scholars tell us that at that time, the word *Ethiopia* probably referred to Egypt.[4] This is confirmed by the fact that the official was reading a book of Jewish scripture, and in those days no Jews were living in the region we now call Ethiopia (then known as "Abyssinia"). Philip offered to help the man interpret what he was reading. He explained how Jesus Christ had come to fulfill Isaiah's prophecies. The official was so moved by the truth that he stopped the chariot and asked Philip to baptize him in a nearby pond.

This man, the people at Pentecost, or other Egyptian Christians soon established a church in Egypt. At this time, the country was ruled by the Ptolemies, who followed the myths and rituals of Greece. The Egyptian church grew slowly during the generations that followed. Despite persecution by the Muslims who later took control of Egypt, the church has survived, and is now called the Coptic church.

Egypt's Future

When we think of how God has dealt with the Egyptians over so many centuries, we ought to pray more fervently than ever that God will bring them to Christ. My missionary friends tell me that Egypt may be on the brink of a mighty renewal for God. That part of the world is very unsettled these days. But if we pray for Egypt, God may yet send a mighty revival upon that land and awaken it to the gospel of Jesus Christ.

We also should take a lesson from Egypt's experience. The people of that country saw repeated demonstrations of God's power, yet they persisted in their godless pagan beliefs. Not only did the Egyptians see miracles such as the ten plagues that God sent to change the pharaoh's mind, they also saw many living examples of God's covenant. They saw how God cares for the people who worship Him. They knew that God was not just some magical force; He is a Person who loves the men and women He creates, and who blesses them when they serve Him. Yet the Egyptians were not convinced to serve Him.

We Americans have had the same kind of opportunities. We have seen God's hand in the history of our nation—how He has guided and prospered our ancestors who trusted Him. If we as a people turn away from Him now to follow exotic cults and philosophies, we will be just as pagan as the Egyptian pharaohs so long ago. It could happen. And if we let it happen, I believe the fate of ancient Egypt will be the fate of America.

5

BABYLONIAN RELIGION:
The Roots of Astrology

After the Flood, the human race began to multiply once again upon earth. God told Noah and his sons the same thing he had told Adam and Eve at the beginning: "Be fruitful, and multiply, and replenish the earth" (Gen. 9:1; cf. Gen. 1:28). That's exactly what they did. Noah's sons—Shem, Ham, and Japheth—led their families out of the ark and began the enormous task of reestablishing human society. Everything had been destroyed by the Flood, so it was their job to start from scratch, building a civilization that would be obedient to God.

Despite the enormity of the task, one of the greatest cultures of the world—the Babylonian Empire—emerged just three generations after the Flood. Even more astounding is the fact that Noah's descendants had turned completely away from God by that time.

Let's follow very carefully the chain of events that took the human race from Ararat to Babylon, from the Flood to apostasy, from true worship to paganism.

The Tower of Babel

Genesis 10:6 begins a long account of the people who descended from Noah. We won't attempt to follow every branch of this genealogy; instead we will focus on those who organized the Babylonian Empire.

One day Noah got drunk with wine and stripped off his clothes. Ham lewdly gazed upon his father's nakedness; then, perhaps feeling guilty, he summoned his brothers to cover Noah. When Noah's head cleared, he realized what Ham had done. He pronounced a curse upon the boy (Gen. 9:25) which, by implication, extended to Ham's descendants as well.

Cush was a son of Ham, and Nimrod was a son of Cush (Gen. 10:6–8). Here the Bible stops the genealogy to tell us that Nimrod "began to be a mighty one in the earth" (v. 8). In the land of Shinar Nimrod founded the first kingdom after the Flood, its major cities being Babel, Erech, Accad, and Calneh (Gen. 10:10). This was the beginning of the Sumerian culture, which preceded the Babylonian Empire.

The people of Nimrod's kingdom decided to build a capital city with a great tower that would reach into the sky. ". . . Let us make us a name," they said to themselves, "lest we be scattered abroad upon the face of the whole earth" (Gen. 11:4).

The Bible says that Noah lived three hundred and fifty years after the Flood (Gen. 9:28), so he may still have been alive when his great-grandson Nimrod began building the tower. I can just imagine the old man walking around the construction site, tears streaming down his cheeks, and saying, "Believe God! Trust God! You don't need a tower to heaven. You need a clean heart."

But Nimrod's people kept on building. They kept on telling themselves that they could do anything and didn't need God's help. The tower was a colossal monument to human pride, an idol to man's own vanity. But it was also a pagan shrine. Thorkild Jacobsen of the Oriental Institute identifies the tower as

> . . . the great ziggurat or stage tower of the Marduk temple in Babylon, Etemenanki, which consisted of six square stages one on top of the other, the last one crowned by a small chapel for the god. The ground plan of this tower was recovered by Koldewey in his excavations in Babylon. . . . In addition we have a description of the tower as it looked in Hellenistic times, given by Herodotus.[1]

(The average reader might not realize this by reading the Scripture text alone. It's another example of how archaeology is helping us understand the background of Bible events.)

The tower of Babel angered God, not only because it symbolized man's rebellious pride, but because it glorified a pagan god. For this reason, God imposed on the builders a multitude of languages, so that they could no longer understand one another. He broke up their conspiracy to live without God.

But He did not rid them of their pride. That sinful element caused Nimrod and his descendants to expand the city of Babylon (Greek form of *Babel*) until it covered an area of at least one hundred square miles.[2] They made it the most magnificent city on the Plain of Shinar.

The Bible tells us that two generations later God "divided" the earth (Gen. 10:25). Obviously, this does not refer to ethnic or language divisions, since God accomplished that at Babel, but scholars disagree about the meaning of this statement. I believe it refers to the division of the continents. Geologists tell us that the earth once had a single land mass (which they call Gondwanaland), and thousands of years ago a series of earthquakes shattered this mass into the continents that we have today. I believe this happened during the time of Peleg. It was God's way of further separating the descendants of Noah to prevent worldwide apostasy.

Three generations later, we find a descendant of Shem named Terah living in Ur, a city southeast of Babylon controlled by the Chaldeans. The Bible says that Terah took his sons Abram and Nahor, along with all of their families, and began a long journey west to the land of Canaan (Gen. 11:31). They took the easiest route, along the lush valley of the Euphrates River. They no doubt passed the city of Babylon, which by now was the strongest fortress of the entire region. They stopped to rest at the town of Haran, in what is now eastern Syria, where Terah died. Soon after, God called Abram to finish the journey to Canaan, where he was to possess the land and begin a great nation (Gen. 12:1–3). This initiated God's dispensation of Promise.

It's important to notice that God was speaking to people who lived in Ur, Haran, and other major cities of Mesopotamia during the time that the Babylonian Empire was being formed. He didn't just reveal Himself to Noah. He didn't just reveal Himself to Nimrod. He revealed Himself in various ways to every generation that lived in this part of the world, but only a few people like Abram responded to Him. The descendants of Noah drifted farther and farther into paganism, which was about to manifest itself in the Babylonian Empire. Only a few of them remained faithful to God.

Babylonian Gods and Myths

The Babylonian Empire first attained prominence under King Hammurabi around 1700 B.C., about three hundred years after Abraham lived. Hammurabi was a genius of civil administration who assembled one of the first written law codes of mankind some two hundred and fifty years before God gave Moses the Ten Commandments. The Babylonian king also organized his nation's religion. He brought together the many pagan myths and traditions that Babylonians had created since the time of Nimrod and attempted to establish a new religious cult that would unify his people. It is impossible to describe many of their myths in this brief chapter. But we should note a couple of them to give some idea of the deep-rooted paganism that existed in Babylon.

Long before Hammurabi, the priests of Babylon developed an elaborate creation story called the *Enuma Elish,* which said that the god Marduk created the world by splitting open a wicked sea monster. They wrote a story about a fictional hero called Gilgamesh, who survived a great flood by playing a trick on the gods. They dreamed up a story about a divine human character named Adapa, caretaker of the city of Eridu, who fouled up the weather because the wind overturned his fishing boat; to get things back in order, the gods had to give the priests of Eridu the power to exorcise demons and cure diseases. I could go on and on; the list of myths seems endless. But this gives some idea of the mess Hammurabi inherited.

Since Hammurabi had a gift for administration and organization, he went to work putting Babylon's religion in to a neat, useful form. He made Marduk, god of the city of Babylon, the national god; he established an annual feast to celebrate Marduk's creation of the world; and he declared himself to be the chief priest of Marduk. In other words, he used the religion to gather political power for himself. Why not? He knew the myths were nothing more than a pack of lies; he could use them any way he wanted.

Of course, the Babylonians had a whole pantheon of gods. They had Shamash, the sun god; Sin, the moon god; Ishtar, the goddess of fertility; and so on. They worshipped natural elements, such as the sky, earth, and water. They imagined strange creatures that were half human and half animal. They worshipped the things of nature, they worshipped their gods, they even worshipped their king. I guess you could say they were the most worshipful people of their time. But they didn't worship the Lord.

The Babylonians believed in numerology and astrology. Their wise men studied the movements of stars and planets, hoping to learn how they could please Marduk and all their other gods.

God's Response

Considering all of this, we might assume that God would give up on the Babylonians. After all, they were Noah's descendants, and their ancestors had worshipped Him. He had every right to abandon them now. But He didn't. Babylon's fortunes rose, fell, and rose again—but God kept trying to reach the nation's people.

In the third chapter of Daniel we read about King Nebuchadnezzar, who came to the throne of Babylon in 604 B.C. This was over one hundred years after Israel fell. Many Jewish people were living in Nebuchadnezzar's empire; the ablest of them served in his royal court. No doubt they told him about the true God who ruled the entire universe, including Babylon. But the king persisted in his paganism.

He ordered his men to erect a large golden statue of himself, which was to be worshipped. He instructed all of his government officials to attend the dedication ceremony and to bow down to the statue. (This fellow had a real ego problem!) But three of his Jewish administrators wouldn't comply, and the king's spies reported this to him. Nebuchadnezzar flew into a rage and ordered the three men—Shadrach, Meshach, and Abed-nego—to appear before him to answer the charges. He threatened to have them thrown into a blazing hot furnace if they didn't worship the image. Their answer is a classic.

> If it be so, our God whom we serve is able to deliver us from the burning fiery furnace, and he will deliver us out of thine hand, O king. But if not, be it known unto thee, O king, that we will not serve thy gods, nor worship the golden image which thou hast set up (Dan. 3:17,18).

What tremendous faith they had! They were willing to stand before this pagan king—undoubtedly the most powerful king in the known world at that time—and defy his orders, so that they could serve their God instead. They said, in effect, "We have no worries, Nebuchadnezzar. We know our God will take us out of the furnace. And even if He decides to let us burn, we still won't worship you."

The king was hopping mad. He ordered his soldiers to stoke the furnace until it was seven times hotter than usual. Then they bound the three men and threw them into the furnace. The fire was so hot that it killed the soldiers who threw them in (v. 22).

But it didn't kill Shadrach, Meshach, and Abednego. In fact, the king saw them calmly walking around on the hot coals, and he saw another man with them, who was "like the Son of God" (v. 25). Nebuchadnezzar asked them to come out, and he found that they weren't harmed at all—they didn't even have a smoky smell about them. He was so impressed that he passed a royal decree that no one could criticize the Jews for worshipping God (v. 29).

Later, Nebuchadnezzar was stricken with a rare form of insanity that caused him to think he was a wild animal. The king left his royal palace and roamed the hillsides of Babylonia as if he were a wild boar rooting for food. He lived that way for seven years, and then God restored him to his right mind and allowed him to resume his office as king. He said,

> Now I Nebuchadnezzar praise and extol and honor the King of heaven, all whose works are truth, and his ways judgment: and those that walk in pride he is able to abase (Dan. 4:37).

You might think this example would have turned the empire to God, but it didn't. Nebuchadnezzar's son, Belshazzar, immersed himself in the pagan traditions of his father, exalting himself as the high priest of the pagan god Marduk and regaling his friends with wild parties. He had his servants bring out the gold and silver cups that once had been used in the temple in Jerusalem to add a more festive touch to his banquet hall. The king and his friends celebrated by drinking toasts to the gods of gold, silver, brass, and so on.

At the moment they were celebrating, a hand appeared over the golden candlesticks they had taken from the temple. The king no doubt gaped, goggle-eyed, while the mysterious hand wrote an inscription on the wall in a language that none of them understood. The party mood left him, and the anxious king called for his astrologers to interpret the strange writing. None of them could do it. His wife suggested that they call Daniel, a young Jewish man who had a gift for interpreting visions and other puzzling phenomena. Daniel came and interpreted the message to read: "God hath numbered thy kingdom, and finished it. . . . Thou art weighed in the balances, and art found wanting. . . . Thy kingdom is divided, and given to the Medes and Persians" (Dan. 5:26–28).

Belshazzar made a great to-do over rewarding Daniel for his services, but he gave no indication of wanting to change his ways. So that very night, thirty-two-year-old Darius, the Mede, seized Belshazzar's temple and killed the pagan king.

The Babylonian Empire was another tragic example of hardened paganism. The people turned from the one true God to create imaginary gods of their own, and even when God confronted them with His presence, they tried to pretend He made no difference to them.

Babylonian Religion Today

Though the Persians destroyed the Babylonian Empire over twenty-five hundred years ago, we would be wrong to suppose that the Babylonian religion was destroyed as well. To my knowledge, no one still worships Marduk and the other characters of Babylonian myths. But thousands of people still follow astrology and numerology, which the Persians absorbed from the religion of Babylon. The heresies and untruths that permeated ancient Babylon have been passed from generation to generation, and they are found in the hearts of many Americans today—including many people who profess to be Christian.

Pick up your daily newspaper, and you'll probably find a set of astrology predictions for the day. Visit your neighborhood supermarket, and you'll find several books on astrology and fortune-telling in the magazine rack or along the check-out counter. These things are available because people ask for them. People use them. People still follow the pagan ideas of Babylon.

If you follow astrology and fortune-telling, you are destined for the same fate as the Babylonians. God judged Babylon and all that Babylon had created, and he found it "wanting." He destroyed the Babylonian Empire because of its deep iniquity, and He will destroy you if you insist on following Babylon's lies.

God was right there in Babylon, speaking to the Babylonians through His servants, but they would not listen. I hope you won't make that mistake.

If you're involved in astrology, fortune-telling, or similar paganistic activities, I hope you will realize that God loves you and that you don't need to sell yourself to these devilish lies to find the right course for your life. God is stretching His arms of love out to you. Just as He showed His love to Noah, He is trying to reach everyone in the world today to say, "I love you. I want to help you."

May we never worship figments of our own imagination. May we never worship the things of our present world. Instead, may we always worship the true, living God who wishes to bless us today.

6

GREECE AND ROME: "Professing to Be Wise . . ."

The ancient Greeks were world-renowned for their wisdom, the Romans for their military might. These two cultures were the guiding lights of the Western world for more than a thousand years and their influence continues to shape the laws, concepts, and customs of most Western peoples today. Yet both of these cultures wrapped themselves in speculative, mystical religions. Despite their love for logic and philosophy, the Greeks and Romans loved mythology just as much. Despite their devotion to law and order, they were just as devoted to a gaggle of capricious, immoral "gods." "Professing themselves to be wise," the apostle Paul said, "they became fools" (Rom. 1:22).

We should take a close look at the religions of these ancient civilizations. I believe they give us a reflection of the attitudes we see in our land today. The Greeks and Romans, like the Egyptians, may be able to warn us of some dangerous trends in our supposedly Christian society.

A Constellation of Deities
Both the Greeks and the Romans were stargazers.

For centuries they lived on farms and in small country villages where there was no leisure-time entertainment to speak of, so they spent much of their free time studying the nighttime sky. They let their imaginations roam. Their storytellers developed a number of legends based on the stars; these legends grew into the vast library of stories that we know as Greek and Roman *mythology*.

These stargazing people imagined that a certain cluster of stars made the shape of a dog. Another cluster made the shape of a hunter. Still another group of stars formed a lion. On and on they went, identifying a host of gods, goddesses, and gigantic beasts that seemed to glitter in the heavens. The Greeks and Romans were very creative people, and they conjured up some very elaborate stories about these characters. They believed that all of these gods were watching them and influencing their thoughts. They thought that some gods had come to earth in human form to play malicious pranks on human subjects. According to mythology, these gods were boisterous, selfish beings who had no moral standards at all. They got drunk, caroused, and enjoyed illicit sex (with other gods or humans) whenever they liked. Perhaps these stories were a kind of wishful thinking for the Greeks and Romans, who may have played out through the "gods" some of the things they secretly wanted to do themselves. These ancient people created dozens of gods; literally "the sky was the limit" so far as their mythology was concerned.

Greek Religion

When Paul visited the Greek capital of Athens, he found that "the city was full of idols" (Acts 17:16, RSV). It was cluttered with statues and temples honoring the many gods that the Greeks had devised over the centuries. Among these was Zeus, the god of the sky, who the Greeks believed to be the father of all gods. Apollo was the sun god, who crossed the heavens in a fiery chariot each day, warming the earth and causing the farmer's crops to grow. Pan was the Greek god of the forests, fields, and meadows, as well as god of the wild animals and flocks. The Greeks imagined him as half man, half goat, with hairy hind legs and hooves.

A great seafaring people, the Greeks believed that Poseidon was god of the sea. Sailors carved the image of Poseidon with his three-pronged spear on the bow of each ship in hopes that he would protect them as they sailed the high seas.

Zeus' wife was Hera, the goddess of women and marriage. Zeus and Hera were said to have a son named Hercules, the famous god of strength and courage. Artemis was the Greek goddess of the moon and the hunt; in some cities of Greece (such as Ephesus), she was worshipped as a fertility goddess. Aphrodite was thought to be the goddess of love and beauty.

The Greeks built beautiful temples for most of their imaginary gods and followed different rituals for worshipping each one. Worship might mean dropping a pinch of incense on the altar fire or having sexual intercourse with a temple "priestess." Some "temples" were little more than glorified massage parlors.

The Greeks believed their gods could protect them. Each city had its own patron god or goddess, and even though the people of that city worshipped all of the gods, they gave a special place to the temple of this god—usually on top of the highest hill in the city. They believed the patron god or goddess would give their armies victory and would never allow the city to fall to its enemies. Athena (goddess of wisdom and craftsmanship) was the patron goddess of Athens; Mars (god of war) was the patron god of Sparta.

Some gods were supposed to have healing powers. The Greeks especially honored the god Asclepius for this reason, and some cities had a special temple area (called the *Aesclepium*) where people could come to ask Asclepius for healing.

The Greeks sought the gods' approval for any important decisions they had to make. They often went to the temple of Apollo at Delphi, where a priestess sat over a gas fissure in the volcanic rocks and muttered unintelligible words of prophecy. Other priests interpreted her words, which were supposed to come from Apollo himself. But the oracle usually gave people vague instructions that could mean almost anything—so that, no matter what happened, the priests could say she was right!

The Greeks believed the gods could give them bountiful crops, artistic skills, or intellectual powers. Each person was careful to worship the god or goddess of his particular vocation. Farmers worshipped Artemis (fertility), poets and philosophers worshipped Athena (wisdom), soldiers worshipped Mars (war), and so on.

It amazes me to think that these people of such high learning—so intelligent that other countries sent their royal children to study in Greek schools—could swallow such ridiculous ideas on religion. These people knew what was happening in the Holy Land. Greek traders had visited Palestine for centuries, and the armies of Alexander the Great toured the whole Middle East in their wars of conquest around 330 B.C. They knew about God's chosen people, the Jews. They knew about the great miracles God had wrought for Abraham, Isaac, Jacob, Moses, David, Elijah, and so many other Jewish leaders. In fact, the Greeks translated the Old Testament into Greek and placed several copies of it in the library of Alexandria. They knew the truth about God. But they kept on believing their silly myths and superstitions, a fact that is hard to fathom.

The Greeks practiced many secret rites to honor their gods. They formed societies and clubs to promote the worship of their favorite gods, and these organizations initiated new members with ritual washings, special instructions, and viewings of sacred cult objects. They did all of these things behind closed doors, often under the cover of darkness. The Greeks considered it a privilege to belong to one of these elite "mystery" religions, with their hidden ceremonies that were supposed to give members vital insights into the secrets of life. Today we have a number of religious organizations that are supposed to fulfill the same function; they are descendants of the Greek "mystery" religions. A little later we will consider some other modern remnants of Greek religion.

Roman Religion

In nearly every area of life, the Romans imitated the Greeks. The Romans were better soldiers and administrators, but when they conquered the Greek territories of the Mediterranean, they immediately started to copy the sophisticated Greeks. They admired Greek art and philosophy; they admired Greek religion just as much. In fact, they adopted most of the Greek gods and myths as their own, giving them Latin names. They called Zeus "Jupiter," Hera "Juno," Athena "Minerva," and so on. They kept most of the Greek myths and added a few of their own.

The Pantheon in Rome, built to house statues of the many different Roman gods, is still one of the most beautiful buildings in the world. This exquisite marble structure shows how important the Romans considered their gods to be; they placed images of the gods in temples more exquisite than the houses of the wealthiest persons in the empire (including the emperor's).

Statues of Roman gods are scattered across the

Mediterranean area. I have found them in the ruins of the Roman cities in Lebanon, in Israel, in Egypt—and, of course, in the capital city of Rome itself. As the Romans expanded their realm, they took their pagan religion with them, forcing the people they conquered to worship as they did.

As the Empire rose to the height of its power, Roman rulers began to think of themselves as gods. When Julius Caesar's grand-nephew Octavian became emperor in 31 B.C., he gave himself the title of *Augustus Caesar* ("magnificent ruler"). His generals and governors flattered the Caesar by telling their subjects to offer sacrifices to him. Augustus and his successors allowed this practice to continue, and by early Christian times the emperors demanded that they be worshipped. Hundreds of Christians were executed because they would not burn incense to the emperor.

Like the Greeks, the Romans had direct contact with the Holy Land. They were familiar with Jewish history. They saw Jesus traveling the roads of Palestine, ministering to all kinds of people, both Jews and Gentiles. And they carried out the Jewish leaders' wishes by having Jesus executed. The Romans stared the Truth right in the face and kept on pretending He wasn't the Truth. They were hardened in their paganism.

All pagan religion is bondage. Pagan people are enslaved to the lies and fears that Satan has planted in their minds. Outwardly they may seem very independent, but inwardly they are serving the devil.

I recently met a young man involved in a pagan cult. I started praying for him. I said, "I want you to come out of it. I want you to give it up."

"Oh, no!" he cried. "I'll be killed if I do."

Paganism gets a firm grip on people. If you've never confronted paganism before, you probably don't realize how powerful it is. But these people know it's a matter of life or death. They know that their pagan friends will try to keep them in the pack, and they know their own inner fears will gnaw at them. It's not easy for them to swim against the tide.

This is the way it was in the Roman Empire. The people who took offense at the pagan religion of the state were still obliged to worship the mythical gods and egotistical emperors of Rome. All of their friends did so, and the law required it. Anyone who cared to take a stand for the truth risked being put to death as a traitor. The early Christians faced this obstacle and kept right on worshipping their Lord. Many of them were martyred in the sports arenas of the great metropolis of Rome.

God's Response

Jesus Christ said, "I am the way, the truth, and the life: no man cometh unto the Father, but by me" (John 14:6). He acknowledged no other god but the Creator of the universe, the Lord God of Abraham, Isaac, and Jacob. He recognized no other priest or mediator between God and man besides Himself.

He presented Himself as the one sufficient Sacrifice for the sins of mankind. He said:

> . . . I have come that they might have life, and that they might have it more abundantly. I am the good shepherd: the good shepherd giveth his life for the sheep (John 10:10,11).

All the absurd myths of the Greek and Roman sages seem even more absurd beside the gospel of Christ. He offered everyone a direct way to the throne of God—the way of repentance and surrender, trusting Christ to cover all sins. Yet the Greeks and Romans preferred their own way of salvation—the way of superstition, idolatry, and mystic rituals.

Before we laugh at them, let's take a serious look at America. I think we find the same kind of irrational behavior here, despite all of God's generous invitations to follow the truth.

More Bibles are published in North America each year than on any other continent of the world. We have more Christian publishing houses, more Christian radio and TV stations, more local churches and pastors than all other nations combined. Yet we have more nominal Christians—people who say they're Christian but don't live like it—than we have genuine, born-again believers.

Several years ago, Pierre Berton wrote a very disturbing book entitled *The Comfortable Pew*. It told about his decision to leave the Anglican church and his growing disgust for all church institutions. Berton wrote:

> The virus that has been weakening the Church for more than a generation is not the virus of anti-religious passion but the very lack of it. . . . The Church to its opponents has become as a straw man, scarcely worth a bullet. . . . Most ministers are scarcely distinguishable by their words, opinions, actions, or way of life from the nominal Christians and non-Christians who form the whole of the community.[1]

I'm afraid he's right. We Americans have tended to take Christianity for granted, and we have used our sophisticated intellects to concoct a myriad of pseudo-religious notions that we follow as if they were the gospel. Many Americans file into church sanctuaries Sunday after Sunday to hear befuddled ministers blather a confused mixture of Scripture, psychology, humanistic philosophy, and advice from Dear Abby. Many of our seminaries send out graduates who aren't sure whether Jesus is the Son of God, whether the Bible is God's inspired Word, or even where to find the Book of Hosea. We have invested tremendous amounts of money and raw human energy in our quest to know the truth about life; all we have found are abstract philosophies, empty symbols, and a perverse kind of self-worship. We have much in common with the Greeks and Romans.

Professing to be wise, we have become fools.

7

HINDUISM

Hinduism is perhaps the most complex and confusing pagan religion in the world today. It is marked by extremes and contradictions, but these don't seem to bother the Hindu worshippers. For example, Hinduism places such a high premium on life that faithful Hindus would never intentionally kill an insect, a predator, or a poisonous snake; yet they let millions of their own people live in abject poverty. Some Hindus withdraw from social circles, while others, such as Mahatma Gandhi, become persuasive politicians with millions of followers. Some Hindus inflict their bodies with terrible pain for religious discipline, while others live sedate, comfortable lives.

We do not know exactly when Hinduism began. Hindus do not revere any one founder or pioneer thinker of their religion, and the first Hindu writings were probably recorded long after the religion began. It seems that Hinduism arose during the dispensation of Law—about the time Moses was leading the Hebrews to the Promised Land. Unlike other pagan religions, Hinduism did not depend on any great leaders for its survival, yet there are about four hundred million Hindus in the world today, nearly twice the number of people living in the United States. Dr. Louis Renou, who has studied Hindu writings for many years, observes:

> No founder's initiative, no dogma, no reform have imposed restrictions on [Hinduism's] domain; on the contrary, the contributions of the centuries have been superimposed without ever wearing out the previous layers of development.[1]

Because of this, the Hindus have many different books of scripture and they respect all of them—even though their scriptures radically disagree. They follow hundreds of different rituals and worship a teeming multitude of gods.

To understand how all of this came about, let us try to look back at the beginnings of Hinduism.

Origins of Hinduism

As we saw earlier, the three sons of Noah—Shem, Ham, and Japheth—started to repopulate the earth after the Flood. Ham's descendants moved south to settle in Arabia and Africa; they developed the religion of animism in all of its various forms. Japheth's descendants moved west to settle in Asia Minor and Europe; they later developed the religions of Greece and Rome. But Shem's descendants went east to Asia and India, where they developed the religions of Hinduism and Islam. When they emerged from the ark, Shem, Ham, and Japheth knew about the love of God through their father

Noah. But in just a few generations, the rebelliousness of human nature led them and most of their descendants away from God.

Paganism became very strong in the East, where Shem's descendants settled. This may be one reason why God did not tell Abraham to go east, but west (Gen. 12:1–5). It may help to explain why God did not allow Paul to enter Asia (Acts 16:6). God knew that His Word would be resisted by the pagan cults that were growing stronger in Asia and India.

Strong warring tribes known as the Indo-Aryans moved into India in the time of Abraham (*ca.* 2000 B.C.). The Indo-Arayans brought to India their language (known as proto-Sanskrit) and their religion, a crude form of animism. They brought hymns, chants, and rituals associated with their worship of nature, and by 1000 B.C. they had recorded many of these hymns in writing. They called these collections of hymns the *Veda* (Sanskrit, "revealed wisdom"). So about the time David was composing the Psalms, the Aryans were composing their religious songs, the Vedas.

About two hundred years later, the priests of this religion began compiling books of doctrine called the *Brahmanas.* They also made a series of handbooks called the *Sutras,* which described their doctrines in a more systematic way. They did this circa 800-600 B.C., about the time Daniel and his friends were witnessing to their conquerors in Babylon.

From about 600 to 300 B.C., the Hindu priests compiled several philosophical books called the

Upanishads (Sanskrit, "to sit down beside"). These primarily were imaginary dialogues between Hindu teachers and their pupils.

Gradually, Hinduism exerted more and more influence over the affairs of government. The royal families who ruled India liked to follow the traditions of their Aryan ancestors, so it was only natural for them to incorporate Hindu ideas into the laws of state. Around 250 B.C., they developed a collection of civic and religious laws called the *Manu* (named for the legendary Manu, the Hindu equivalent of Adam).

Still later, about the time of Christ, some Hindu writer composed a long epic poem known as the *Bhagavad-Gita,* which describes a battle between a man named Arjuna and his charioteer, Krishna. In the course of their struggle, the poem reveals that Krishna was the god Vishnu, who took human form to offer salvation to anyone who would surrender his life to Krishna. Because this seems so similar to the gospel of Jesus Christ, some scholars call the *Bhagavad-Gita* the "New Testament of Hinduism."[2] Of course, nothing could be farther from the truth; a fictitious god like Krishna can't do anything to save us. Yet the Hindus were talking about this at the same time the real Savior was walking the streets of Jerusalem. Was that just a coincidence? I don't think so.

Still later, Hindu wise men compiled books called the *Puranas* (Sanskrit, "ancient tales"), which described the myths of Rama, Krishna, and other gods. These stories are very popular among Hindu people today.

Key Hindu Beliefs

Because Hinduism has so many scriptures and so many contradictory beliefs, it is hard to sort out any teachings that are common to all Hindu people. But there are some doctrines that seem to be accepted by most Hindus, doctrines that are mentioned in most of their different scriptures.

Atman ("breath")—Hindus believe that every living thing has an essential life or soul, which they call the *atman*. The word literally means "breath." They believe every person has a soul, every animal has a soul, every tree and blade of grass has a soul. They think that every soul is just a small part of a great cosmic Soul, and for this reason, every living thing is holy and should not be harmed.

Karma ("to create")—Hindus believe that every living thing has a purpose, a mission, or a vocation; in other words, every living thing has a given function. This task is that being's *karma*. If a person, animal, or plant fulfills its *karma* properly, that being can return to life in a more sophisticated form. For example, a spider that does a good job of being a spider may be reborn as a cat, while a man who does a poor job of being a man may be reborn as a snail.

Samsara ("to cross over, wander")—This process of being reborn over and over again is called *samsara*. The Hindus believe that every person has lived several lives before the current one. They believe one is destined to keep on being reborn until he loses all selfish ambitions and yields himself completely to the cosmic Soul (Atman). Then, when the person dies, he will gain release from *samsara* and be absorbed into the cosmic Soul.

These doctrines—particularly the doctrine of *samsara*—place the Hindus in a horrible kind of spiritual slavery. They believe that all creatures are of the same essence, that is, the only differences between a mouse and a king are their outward appearances and their missions in life. But this is wrong. God made men and women in His own image (Gen. 1:27), unlike any other creature on the face of the earth. "So we thy people and sheep of thy pasture will give thee thanks for ever . . ." (Ps. 79:13). We are created more wondrously than any other living thing, with the freedom to praise God for His gracious love.

The Hindu doctrines have given India the awful caste system. The Indian government has tried unsuccessfully to destroy the caste system by law, but it endures because it is a natural result of the people's religion. India's society is divided into five major castes—the Brahmins (priestly caste), the Satriyas (military and administrative caste), the Vaisyas (trade caste), the Sudras (peasant caste), and the "untouchables."

> If the caste theory is observed, there are few details of existence which are not affected by membership in a caste and few traits of caste which are not definitely of a religious significance.[3]

87

Gods of Hinduism

As difficult as it is to identify the doctrines of Hinduism, it is even more difficult to identify its gods. The Hindus are said to have over three million gods. When you visit the Hindu places of worship and see the endless variety of idols and images, that figure seems altogether reasonable. Hindu legends tell of many, many gods, but a few gods are mentioned more than the rest:

Shiva is a dancing figure with four arms. He is the god of destruction. Hindus recognize Shiva in any destructive event, such as a hurricane, an earthquake, or even a political uprising.

Vishnu, the god of the sun, is thought to be the preserver of all things. Hindus believe that Vishnu has come to earth in human form at several times in history.

Brahma, the god of creation, is largely ignored in the Hindu religion. Hindus seem to think that his work was finished long ago and there's no need to pay particular attention to him now.

Brahman is supposed to be the "Divine Ground," the spirit that enlivens all other gods. Hindus say that Shiva, Vishnu, and Brahma are just different expressions of Brahman. Liberal anthropologists have seized on this fact to try to "prove" that Hindus have a divine trinity as do Christians. In fact, the Hindus have a divine *multiplicity,* because they believe that Brahman expresses itself through all of the thousands (maybe millions) of gods that they worship. This is utter paganism.

Hindus define *yoga* as any method of finding union with the Divine Ground or Brahman, Yoga may involve long periods of meditation, chanting, bodily exercise, or self-inflicted suffering. A person who devotes his life to yoga is called a *yogi*.

Of course, most Americans think that "yoga" is only a method of physical exercise. They don't realize that the Hindus developed these exercises as a way to find spiritual salvation. Yoga is a pagan ritual that many Westerners follow because it makes them feel "more relaxed."

Demonic Influence

Pagan worshippers are demon worshippers, whether they realize it or not. Perhaps nowhere is this more evident than in Hinduism.

For example, I once witnessed a Hindu funeral for a cow. Hindus believe the cow is a very sacred animal. Gandhi said, "To protect the cow is to protect the whole dumb creation of earth." Another Hindu writer says, "The cow is of all animals the most sacred. Every part of its body is inhabited by deity. Every hair on its body is inviolate."

So when a cow dies, Hindus stage a great celebration. I saw them put garlands of flowers around the neck and hoofs of the cow's carcass and gingerly lift it onto the funeral bier. The people sang and danced through the streets. Many of them fell to the ground, writhing uncontrollably. They were obviously under demonic power.

Even though Hinduism teaches its followers to

renounce self and become part of the cosmic Soul, strict Hindus are very proud. They feel godlike and are interested only in their own progress. Krishna is supposed to have said:

Die, and you win heaven. Conquer, and you enjoy the earth. . . . Realize that pleasure and pain, gain and loss, victory and defeat, are all one and the same: then go into battle. Do this and you cannot commit any sin.[4]

This kind of attitude does not come from God; it comes from Satan. Like other pagan religions, Hinduism is inspired by Satan and controlled by his demonic influences.

Hinduism and the Gospel

I have visited India many times to hold evangelistic campaigns and carry out missionary work. I know that it is very difficult to turn Hindu people back to God, but we must keep on trying.

According to legend, the apostle Thomas went to India and established the first Christian church nearly two thousand years ago. A Christian witness has been present in India and other Hindu countries longer than in most other parts of the world. And don't forget that God revealed His truth to many people in the Middle East at the same time the Hindus turned against God; He was not hiding Himself.

God loves Hindu people, so we should love them. God wants to save Hindu people, so we should want to save them. Some missionaries have felt "put off" by the Hindu's cold response, but we should not abandon these people to paganism. Veteran missionary Harold R. Cook writes:

> . . . There are non-Christian countries today, such as India, who would like to have many of the social services of Christian missions like doctors and hospitals. But they object to evangelism. They don't want the people converted to the Christian faith. And this is quite understandable. What is harder to understand is those Christians who try to separate the two things. They . . . try to help a famished people by giving them food, but neglect to give them the seed. . . . Can it be that they don't see the close connection between the Hindu religion and the pitiful condition of so many of the people?[5]

Most people in India, Sri Lanka, Guyana, and other Hindu countries live in ghastly conditions of filth and starvation. Their misguided religion has made them apathetic about themselves and their fellowman. They accept misery as their *karma* and just keep on suffering. But these people are God's children just as much as we Americans, the Europeans, or the people of any other prosperous area of the world. We have a duty to share food, clothing, and shelter—and also the gospel—to keep them from falling into worse misery.

Hinduism on Our Doorstep

Hinduism is not just a foreign religion; it is now very active in our own country. In fact, it is one of the most popular pagan religions in America. Western civilization first came into contact with Hinduism when the Greek army of Alexander the Great reached India in 323 B.C. The Greeks married hundreds of Hindu women and brought them, along with their Hindu beliefs, back to Greece.

Christian missionaries visited India for centuries, and the church grew slowly in that Hindu culture. During the eighteenth and nineteenth centuries, British scholars took a keen interest in Hinduism and began translating Hindu texts into English, thinking that Hinduism was an exotic novelty.

As the speed of travel and communication increased, Hinduism spread throughout the Western world. Great Britain and America became involved in India's struggle for modernization; names like Gandhi and Nehru became household words. American housewives took up yoga exercises. College students wore Nehru jackets. Fashion designers copied the Indian *sari*. At the same time, Hindu religion was gradually penetrating Western thought. Yogis began translating more Hindu writings into English and sending them to publishers in the United States and Britain.

In 1965, a yogi named Shrila Prabhupada arrived in New York to spread the message of Hinduism in America. He established a nonprofit organization called the International Society of Krishna Consciousness—more commonly known as Hare Krishna. In 1968 he began a farm commune in West Virginia, and in 1972 he opened a Hindu elementary school in Dallas. He built guest centers in India, where his well-to-do followers could relax while they visited the shrines of their "holy land." He chartered his own publishing house in 1972, with offices in Los Angeles, New York, London, and Bombay. It is now producing thousands of copies of his books on Hare Krishna each year. An editor for that publishing house recently commented:

> Under [the yogi's] careful guidance, the Society has grown within a decade to a worldwide confederation of almost 100 *ashramas,* schools, temples, institutes and farm communities.
>
> . . . Inspired by the success of New Vrindavana, now a thriving farm community of more than 1,000 acres, his students have since founded several similar communities in the United States and abroad.
>
> . . . Shrila Prabhupada's most significant contribution, however, is his books. Highly respected by the academic community for their authoritativeness, depth, and clarity, they are used as standard textbooks in numerous college courses. . . .[6]

What began as idle curiosity is turning into widespread discipleship. Thousands of young people have shaved their heads and donned the white robes of the Krishna movement, hoping to find their place in the cosmic Soul of the Hindus.

But Hinduism rejects Jesus Christ as the Son of God. It denies that there is only one God, the Creator and Father of us all. It repudiates the gospel of salvation through Jesus' death on the cross and tells people to save themselves through their *karma*. Whether it appears in the form of Hare Krishna or something else, Hinduism is paganism.

I pray that God will turn the Hindu people back to Him. We should not harden our hearts against any people on earth—Hindu or otherwise—because God loves them just as much as He loves us. We must do everything we can to take the message of salvation to our Hindu neighbors overseas and here at home.

8

BUDDHISM

We are witnessing a tremendous resurgence of Buddhism throughout the world. It is gaining strength not only in Asia, where Buddhism has been known for many centuries, but in Europe, America, and other regions where it is a newcomer. We ought to get acquainted with the teachings of this pagan religion to see how we should respond to it.

Buddhism has cropped up in the headlines several times in the past decade, demonstrating the effect it can have on the lives of men and women. Buddhist priests set themselves afire in the streets of Vietnam to protest the political policies of that country. In Japan, Buddhist sects have aggressively recruited new converts since World War II, using methods much like those of Christian evangelists. In the United States, Buddhism has proven to be more than an intellectual pastime. Buddhist monks walk the streets of our largest cities, begging for food; Buddhist professors teach their religion in many of our state universities. I understand there are more than two hundred thousand Buddhists in the United States today, and their numbers are growing each month. There are estimated to be between 250 and

300 million Buddhists in the world today—more than the total population of the United States. Obviously, this religion exerts a powerful influence on the affairs of Asian countries and on several Western nations as well.

Missionaries find that Buddhism is more hostile to the gospel than is any other major religion. Buddhist families will disown anyone who attends a church service or Bible study. They see Christianity as a major threat. Why? What is there about the gospel that frightens the Buddhists? Where was God when this pagan religion began?

"The Enlightened One"

Buddhism was founded by a Hindu man named Siddhartha Gautama, the son of an Indian rajah. Gautama's family was part of the wealthy military caste, and his father owned a beautiful estate in southern Nepal, near the Himalaya Mountains, where Gautama was born in 624 B.C.

Gautama lived during the time of Confucius— another well-known pagan philosopher—and of Ezekiel, who prophesied the ruin of God's sinful people in Judah. Think about that for a moment: Gautama was born during the time that Ezekiel had contact with God, saw visions of God, and spoke on behalf of God. How can we suppose that God would reveal Himself to a leader in Palestine but hide Himself from a leader in India? That doesn't make sense. Gautama was seeking the truth about life, and the Bible says that God "is a rewarder of them that diligently seek Him" (Heb. 11:6).

Don't be too hasty to blame God because Gautama failed to find Him. Either Gautama wasn't genuinely seeking the truth, or else he found the truth and refused to accept it. God was just as ready to reveal Himself to a rich boy in the hills of India as to a preacher in the pasture lands of Judah. God was in both places.

Legend says that a spirit told Gautama's father that the boy would become a world ruler or a famous philosopher. Being a dyed-in-the-wool military man, Gautama's father did everything he could to keep the boy from seeing human misery or death; he knew that sort of thing had prompted many a youth to become a yogi. But one day Gautama rode his horse to the far reaches of his father's estate. Along the way, he saw an elderly man, a cripple, a corpse, and a wandering Hindu yogi. These hard realities of life made a deep impression on the young man. He decided to leave his wife and family to become a yogi, so he could try to understand why there must be suffering in the world.

For six years, Gautama wandered through the villages of Nepal and northern India, fasting and torturing himself like the other yogis. But this brought him no closer to the truth. Finally, he sat down under a bo tree in the village of Buddh Gaya and resolved not to get up until he found an answer. He stayed there for forty-nine days. At last he found "the bless of liberation," or *Nirvana*. The answer, he decided, was contained in four simple statements that Buddhists now call the Four Noble Truths:

1. Existence brings suffering.
2. The cause of suffering is the desire for pleasure.
3. The way to escape from suffering is to get rid of the desire for pleasure.
4. The way to be rid of desire is to discipline one's mind and to live correctly.

Gautama decided that it was best for a person to seek the "middle way" between pleasure-seeking and self-torture, living pretty comfortably while still focusing the mind on the quest for truth. Two merchants passing through the village heard Gautama's ideas and decided to become his disciples. He later preached to five Hindu monks who had traveled with him and ordained them as the first monks of his new religion. They called Gautama the *Buddha* (Sanskrit, "enlightened one").

Buddhist Teachings

Buddha taught his followers a system of high moral standards so they could achieve "right living." Some of these teachings remind me of the Book of Proverbs. They are practical instructions that show how to live in moderation and treat other people graciously. But many of Buddha's teachings run counter to the revealed will of God.

When a Westerner visits a Buddhist country, he

realizes that Buddhism places great emphasis on its worship rituals. Buddhists imagine that thousands of spirits inhabit the *pagoda,* or temple of worship. So worshippers bring offerings of food, wine, and incense to appease these spirits. Each pagoda contains grotesque images of the gods of Buddhist folklore. There are angry gods, ugly gods, frightening gods. I saw one image of a god with a broken hand; another was portrayed as a poor, emaciated spirit. Buddhists fall down and worship these images, which obviously were made under the inspiration of demons.

A recent issue of *Newsweek* magazine told of a Buddhist temple in Japan where worshippers pray to die. Elderly or sick Buddhists come to this pagoda and pay 2,000 yen (about $8.00) for the privilege of asking their gods to give them death. The temple can offer rites for about a hundred worshippers each hour. This shows the ungodly extremes of Buddhist doctrine. It teaches that the gods can be manipulated for virtually any purpose, and prayer itself is a mechanical exercise. It's like saying, "Put in a quarter and get what you want."

While I was visiting Tibet, I often slept in Buddhist temples. (There was nowhere else to sleep.) One of these temples had ten thousand plaster-of-Paris idols; Buddhist worshippers offered money to some of these images to gain purification and release from suffering. I pointed to the contorted face of one idol and asked a temple priest, "Can this god really help me?"

"I don't know," he replied. "You'd have to believe."

"Well, then, can it help you?"

The priest pondered that question for a moment. "Normally, an idol cannot help me," he said. "But see this hole in its back? This is where the spirit of the idol goes in and out. If I place a gift in front of the idol and pray, the spirit may enter and grant what I ask."

This is demon worship. The Buddhist priest himself admits that the idol is nothing; he is worshipping the capricious spirit that may enter it. The prophet Habakkuk said:

> What profiteth the graven image that the maker thereof hath graven it; the molten image, and a teacher of lies, that the maker of his work trusteth therein, to make dumb idols? Woe unto him that saith to the wood, Awake; to the dumb stone, Arise, it shall teach! Behold, it is laid over with gold and silver, and there is no breath at all in the midst of it (Hab. 2:18,19).

An idol is not holy because it is worshipped. No matter how many people offer sacrifices to it and bow down to it, an idol is still an idol. It is representative of man's rebellion against God. This is the most blatant pagan practice of the Buddhist religion, and it exposes Buddhism for what it really is—a worship of evil spirits.

Buddhist priests and intellectuals aren't very interested in worshipping images; they are more intent upon following Buddha's rules for "right living." Buddhist idol worship, the most popular form of Buddhist worship, developed long after Buddha died. The average Buddhist worships the images in his local shrine, offers incense on the altar, and drops some money in the offering box. So far as he's concerned, that's all he needs to do to achieve "right living." His priests will tackle the more disciplined form of life.

This brings us to the heart of Buddha's teaching—the Eightfold Path of conduct that enables a person to rid himself of human desire. According to Buddha, a person can free himself from the bondage of desire by practicing these eight things:

1. Right views
2. Right aspirations
3. Right speech
4. Right conduct
5. Right livelihood
6. Right endeavor
7. Right mindfulness
8. Right meditation

Obviously, this is a system of mental discipline and practical morality—a system of human works. Buddha believed that anyone who masters the Eightfold Path can escape from the endless cycle of reincarnation that his Hindu masters had explained to him. The Eightfold Path would lead a person to

Nirvana, the total annihilation of self. A person who achieves Nirvana is supposed to be absorbed into the cosmic Soul to which the Hindus refer, reunited with the central spirit of the universe. Tradition says that these were Buddha's dying words:

> My age is now ripe,
> My life draws to its close:
> I leave you, I depart,
> Relying on myself alone!
> Be earnest then, O brethren,
> Holy, full of thought!
> Be steadfast in resolve!
> Keep watch o'er your own hearts!
> Who wearies not,
> But holds fast to his truth and law,
> Shall cross this sea of life,
> Shall make an end of grief.[1]

The Buddhist way of salvation is a self-effort that ends in absolute frustration. No sinner can save himself from sin. No mortal can give himself immortality. Yet Buddha taught that his disciples could work out their own salvation by following the Eightfold Path. He adopted the Hindu idea of reincarnation; he said that a person is born, reborn, and born again until he is able to master the Eightfold Path. Only then does he find release from the cycle of human misery.

Pastor H. S. Vigeveno of Hollywood once had a long conversation with a Buddhist priest in that city, trying to learn what these people believe. The conversation rambled so much that it was hard for Pastor Vigeveno to pin down what the Buddhist was saying, but after he left the meeting, he jotted down the basic ideas as he perceived them:

> Man is his own savior. He achieves enlightenment, eventually. He earns his own rewards, and they will bring him to heaven (Nirvana). So man works his way to God. Grace does not really set him free.[2]

That's Buddhism in a nutshell. It's a religious-sounding philosophy of self-fulfillment, an effort to "pull yourself up by your own bootstraps." But no one has ever been able to save himself. No one ever will. Only the blood of Jesus Christ can cleanse us of our sins. His death on the cross accomplished everything that needs to be accomplished. Self-salvation is a lie.

The idea of reincarnation is an illusion supporting the lie. Many people imagine that they have had certain experiences before; they're sure they've seen a certain street or met a certain person in another life. This is just imagination at work. Many places look similar, and many people look similar. But you live your life only once; there's no second or third chance to do what you ought to do.

God made you an individual. You have one-of-a-kind talents and opportunities that you will never have the chance to use again. The question is, "Will you use them to serve God or to satisfy yourself?" The Bible says, ". . . It is appointed unto men once to die, but after this the judgment" (Heb. 9:27). That leaves no room for reincarnation. We have one life, one choice of how to live that life, and one time of judgment when life is over. There is no time to experiment with exotic ideas about how we can save ourselves. We need to face the truth head-on: Jesus Christ provides our only way to be saved.

> ... The Buddhists' starting point is the nonexistence of personality and the need for obliterating the deceptive appearances of what we call personal human life. In 1 John 2:17 . . . one may find a parallel to the Buddhist belief in the transiency of all matter, but the latter part of the same verse ("but he that doeth the will of God abideth for ever") separates one from Buddhism by ideological light years.[3]

The Christian and the Buddhist would agree that life is brief and full of suffering. But we reject the Buddhist's solution to this problem. Right views, right aspirations, right conduct—plus all of the other things required by the Eightfold Path—will not rid us of the cause of our suffering. Suffering comes from sin, and the only way to be rid of suffering is to be rid of sin. The only way to be rid of sin is to claim Jesus Christ as our all-sufficient Sacrifice for sin. There are not eight ways to salvation, only one: Jesus.

Where Was God?

Buddha lived about the time God was bringing the Jews back to Israel after eighty years of slavery in Babylon. God raised up courageous leaders like

Ezra and Nehemiah to proclaim His Word to the people and to persuade King Cyrus to let them return to the Promised Land. God was at work. So before we say, "Pity, poor Buddha; he didn't know any better," we ought to ask ourselves *why* he didn't know any better. We may find out that he did know better, but decided to "do his own thing."

The Bible says that God reveals Himself to all people who seek Him. "For God giveth to a man that is good in his sight wisdom, and knowledge, and joy . . ." (Eccl. 2:26). "It is the spirit in a man, the breath of the Almighty, that makes him understand" (Job 32:8, RSV). God asked Job, "Who hath put wisdom in the inward parts? or who hath given understanding to the heart?" (Job 38:36). The answer, of course, is God Himself.

God created Gautama, just as He created the prophets of Israel. He endowed "the enlightened one" with the same opportunities that He gave the prophets. We do not know whether God ever revealed Himself to Gautama in a vision, as He did to Jacob. But His Word says that He is "a rewarder of them that diligently seek him" (Heb. 11:6), so we have no reason to doubt that God revealed Himself to Gautama if His presence was truly sought.

Here is how an early Buddhist manuscript described Gautama as he began his search for enlightenment.

This monarch having subdued his passions, his enemies, felt no inclination for such profits as are to be blamed when enjoyed, but was with his whole heart intent on promoting the happiness of his subjects. Holding virtuous practice to be the only purpose of his actions, he behaved like a *Muni* [holy man].

For he knew . . . that people set a high value on imitating the behaviour of the highest. For this reason, being desirous of bringing about salvation for his subjects, he was particularly attached to the due performance of his [Hindu] religious duties.[4]

This indicates that Gautama wanted to find the way of salvation; he wanted to know the truth about life and death. He was diligently seeking to know God, and therefore God must have revealed Himself to Gautama.

We find evidence of this in Buddha's moral teachings. As I mentioned earlier, Buddha taught his followers decent standards of right and wrong, much like the standards we find in the Old Testament. Only God could have revealed these standards to him.

While I was visiting Tibet, I asked a Buddhist man what he would do if he found his neighbor in bed with his wife.

"I would kill him," the Buddhist said.

"Why?" I asked.

"Because it's wrong."

"How do you know it's wrong?" I asked.

"Because my heart tells me so."

"Well, what if your best friend broke into your

house and stole your money? What would you do?"

"I would kill him," the Buddhist said again.

"Why?"

"Because it's wrong. . . ."

I tested him on nearly all of the Ten Commandments, and found that he knew right from wrong—even though he had never heard the name of Jesus. God had planted deep within his conscience a knowledge of good and evil, holy and profane, godly and ungodly. He knew the standard before I ever talked with him. I'm sure the same was true of Buddha twenty-five hundred years ago. God let him choose faith or paganism, and Gautama chose paganism.

Buddhism and the Gospel

Most Americans do not realize how Buddhists are responding to the gospel in foreign lands. Buddhist priests have adopted many methods of Christian evangelism to win new converts. Eugene A. Nida, former secretary for translations with the American Bible Society, came back from Thailand with this report.

Communists claim that their philosophy will be the creed of the future era, while saffron-robed Buddhist priests rally young people in festivals, Sunday Schools, and discussion groups. With hymns such as "Onward Buddhist Soldiers" and "Silent Night, Holy Night" (depicting the birth of Buddha), they diligently instruct the people in social responsibility and new ways of earning merit.[5]

Newspaper reports show that Buddhists in Japan now hold divine healing services where they pray for Buddha to heal sick people. They have started many new Buddhist elementary and secondary schools to indoctrinate their children. One prominent Buddhist sect, the Soka Gakkai, has its own political party that is gradually gaining seats in Japan's parliament. The leaders of this sect have vowed to make Japan a Buddhist state, in the same way that Iran is a Muslim state.

Christian missionaries face a tough challenge in Buddhist countries. This religion has imbedded itself so deeply in the culture of Japan, Korea, Thailand, and other countries that the people view Christian converts as traitors to their heritage. Families disown them; some employers refuse to hire them; some colleges will not enroll them. A Buddhist pays a high price for accepting Jesus Christ as his Savior.

The majority of Buddhists have a distorted view of Christianity, which is why many of them close their minds to the gospel. One day I was talking with a young banker in Hong Kong and asked, "Are you a Christian?"

His eyes twinkled. "No," he replied. "I escaped."

"What do you mean by that?" I asked.

"Oh, I went to a Christian school for twelve years, and I haven't been back since I graduated. I escaped from all that."

"You mean to say that you didn't believe what

they taught you all those years, while you were getting a free education?"

"I got a free education," he agreed. "But I am a Buddhist. I escaped from them."

This young man will have to answer to God for his decision. He had an opportunity to hear about Christ for twelve years, but he acted as though it made no difference. He paid no attention while the Bible was being read. He thought his Christian teachers were jail wardens, and he was proud to say he "escaped" from them. This is a common Buddhist reaction to what the missionaries are doing.

Nevertheless, we must present the gospel to these people. A man once told missionary William Carey, "When God wants to convert the heathen, He'll do it without your help or mine!" But God doesn't give us that luxury. Remember, He told Ezekiel that He would hold us accountable for the lives of pagan people we can reach (Ezek. 3:18). Buddhists are such a people. Their religion has no power to save them, and they are depending on us to tell them about Jesus Christ, the only One who can give them eternal truth, eternal joy, and eternal life.

In spite of their resistance, some Buddhists will give a hearing to the gospel. We need to reach these people. I once visited a Buddhist shrine in Indonesia that had an enormous image of a god with fifty hands. This idol had arms coming out of his chest, arms coming out of his side, and arms coming out of his arms! I guess you could say he was the "handiest'' god I'd ever seen! I walked over to the priest who cared for the shrine, and said, "I see a problem here."

"What is it?" he asked.

"One of the hands has fallen off your god," I said. "But that's all right. I'll just wait for a moment. I'm sure the hand will heal itself. After all, a god with fifty hands must be very powerful."

The priest shook his head and said, "No, sir. I made that god myself in the workshop. I will have to repair that hand."

I placed my hand on the priest's shoulder, looked him straight in the eye, and said, "Sir, let me tell you something: My God made *you*."

I could feel the priest tremble. He looked away.

It was a moment I shall never forget.

9

SHINTOISM

The people of Japan have a saying: "You can live a Buddhist, but you must die a Shintoist." The religion of Shinto is so deeply ingrained in the culture of Japan that most Japanese people practice Shinto rituals, even though they may pay lip service to some other religion. Shinto is the chief religion of Japan, with about sixty-five million adherents. It does not get as much international publicity as Buddhism, but it still should be considered the state religion of Japan.

Actually, Shinto is the old ancestral religion that the people of the Japanese islands were practicing when Buddhist missionaries arrived from China sometime in the sixth century A.D. The rise of Buddhism forced Shinto worshippers to organize their religion more carefully. They prescribed the sacrifices that should be made at certain shrines, how a person should honor the spirits of his dead parents, and so on. Obviously, the Japanese people love and respect Shinto, because it has survived alongside Buddhism for more than thirteen hundred years.

Shinto Teachings

Shinto is a Chinese word meaning "the way of the gods." Japanese people gave this name to their religion to set it apart from Buddhism, which they considered to be an inferior foreign religion. Basically, Shinto is the worship of dead ancestors and the spirits of nature. It is a sophisticated form of animism.

> [Shinto] has a complex pantheon of *kami,* or deities, the most exalted of whom is the sun-goddess known as Ruler of Heaven. Other objects of veneration include deified emperors, guardian family spirits, national heroes, and the divinities of trees, rivers, villages, and water sources.
>
> Shrines ranging from small wayside god-houses to great national sanctuaries have been constructed and dedicated to these deities. Each Shinto home also has a "god-shelf" on which is placed a miniature shrine holding . . . the names of beloved ancestors.[1]

I have passed by many Japanese houses late at night and heard the beating of drums and the playing of other instruments as families worshipped the spirits of their ancestors. Such sounds sent a chill over me. I knew these people were worshipping pagan spirits, and I could feel the power of Satan so strongly that it made me want to hurry along.

Ancestor worship is an important part of the Shinto religion. When a young Japanese person accepts Christ, his parents are likely to say, "Who will pray for me after I'm dead?" They don't care if their children become Buddhists or Muslims or take up any other pagan religion, but they know that Christians will not pray to dead ancestors. Japanese parents may tell their children, "You were born to pray for me when I am gone to the other side. You must ask the gods to help me. That is why you must follow Shinto."

A Shinto shrine is often built over the spot where a famous ancestor died or where an important event took place. Worshippers will come there to burn incense and hang up prayer scrolls, asking the gods to care for the spirits of the dead.

This is why hero worship is so important in Japan. When Japan was at the height of its military power in World War II, soldiers visited the shrines of famous soldiers before they left for battle. Their generals told them that if they gave their lives for Japan, they would join the spirits of the mighty soldiers of the past. In fact, a team of suicide pilots known as the *kamikaze* ("divine wind") flew planes loaded with explosives into American ships. They had been told that they would become gods for being so brave.

These pagan ideas have infected the Japanese culture so deeply that it is hard to change the people's minds. I was visiting Japan in 1936 when King George V of England died. I was sitting in the home of a Japanese pastor one evening, discussing news of the king's death.

"Well," I said, "kings have to die, too. They are human like the rest of us."

The pastor angrily jumped to his feet. "That is not true!" he shouted. "Perhaps this George of England was a man, but our emperor descended from the gods!"

"But you are a Christian," I said.

"Yes, I am a Christian. But you don't take that away from me," he said. "I too have descended from the gods."

I shook my head and said, "I don't believe what I'm hearing."

"I am telling you what I believe."

"Then if I were you I would give up this thing you call Christianity, because it is not the gospel. Your emperor did not descend from the gods. He is not a god, and he will not be a god after he is dead. If he doesn't serve God, he will die and go to hell."

"I don't accept that," my pastor friend said. "I don't believe it."

We lost our friendship that night, because this Japanese pastor was still a Shintoist at heart. After World War II, Shintoism was no longer designated the official state religion, and I thank God for that. But most Japanese people still follow Shinto customs. They are raising the children to worship the spirits of their ancestors, just as their parents and grandparents taught them to do.

Pilgrimage is another important feature of Shintoism. The Japanese people have erected Shinto shrines all across the country, honoring thousands of their ancestors. Every time I go to Japan, I see school children at these shrines, their teachers telling them what happened at these spots and why they should worship there. When they grow up, these children will travel from shrine to shrine, offering sacrifices to the spirits of people they have known or admired.

Shintoists suffered a keen setback in World War II; the religion that rallied their nation to war was not enough to bring victory, and General Douglas MacArthur ordered the new Japanese government to cut off all financial support to Shinto shrines. For a while, some Shintoists gave their allegiance to Christianity because it was the religion of their conquerors, but in recent years these people have turned back to their Shinto customs. One expert in the field of Japanese religion says:

> This movement is not dissimilar to German Nazism in its narrow nationalism and emphasis upon a sacred soil and people. It does not, however, appear to have much future in the face of other movements, such as socialism, communism, and materialism. . . .[2]

I would disagree. History shows that Shinto has been able to borrow strength from new religious and social movements that come into Japan, usually becoming stronger because of them. I think it is too early to write off Shintoism as a dying religion.

God's Response

God has a word for the followers of Shinto. It's the same message Paul and Silas gave to the Philippian jailer: "Believe on the Lord Jesus Christ, and thou shalt be saved, and thy house" (Acts 16:31). God loves all the people of the world because He made them all. He is going to send Jesus back to earth to gather all the people who are faithful to Him and take them to live with Him forever. The Shintoists and Buddhists have a chance to join the great family of God, just as we Americans do. We ought to pray that these people will listen to the gospel, read the prophecies of the Bible, and accept God's offer of eternal life.

"The Lord is . . . not willing that any should perish, but that all should come to repentance" (2 Pet. 3:9). God hears the prayer of a repentant Shinto worshipper just as easily as He hears the prayer of a backsliding Christian. He is just as willing to forgive the sin of someone who has spent his life in paganism as He is to forgive the sin of a young person raised in a godly Christian home. God loves the pagan world; He sent His Son to die for pagans like you and me. Never forget that.

I believe that the grace of God can cut through the traditions that hang like a veil over the face of Shinto worshippers. Pray with me that God will continue speaking to them.

America's Brand of Shintoism

You've probably read all this and said, "So what? Why should I care about the pagan in Japan?"

For two reasons: First, you ought to care because Christians should care about *all* people who do not know Jesus Christ as their personal Savior. Even though they're halfway around the world, Shintoists are important to us because they need to hear the gospel, and we are responsible for taking it to them.

Second, you ought to care about Shintoism because it reminds us of a subtle form of paganism in America today. For lack of a better term, I'll call it "the Americanized gospel." This is the distorted notion that America is God's chosen nation, His special people, and He will protect us no matter what we do.

I've heard many Christians laugh at the serious predicament of America in the Middle East and other parts of the world. They say, "God will work it out. He always has." Friends, I have news for you—God is no country's patriot. No nation carries God in its hip pocket. A nation will enjoy God's blessings only as long as its people obey Him and honor Him, but He plays no favorites with people that live like heathen. Elton Trueblood says,

> It is ridiculous to talk about the "Japanese God" or the "white man's God" or the "American God." These are logical absurdities. . . . What *we* happen to think about God is not very important; what God truly *is* is all-important.[3]

Think about it for a moment. Are you searching the Scriptures to find what God has to say, or are you just going along with what your friends say is "sound doctrine"? Do you have a vital, day-by-day, personal relationship with Jesus Christ, or are you coasting along on the Christian upbringing that your parents gave you? Are you on your knees praying for God to help America and its leaders, or do you suppose that He's going to help us anyway?

You may find out that you're an American-style Christian on the outside, but an American-style Shintoist on the inside. Don't laugh. American "Shintoism" is just as pagan as Japanese Shintoism.

Only God is the One we should worship. Not country, not family, not tradition. Only God.

10

CONFUCIANISM AND TAOISM:
Humanistic Religions

Chinese sages like to tell an old story about a conversation between the philosopher Confucius and his son. They say that Confucius met his son one morning and asked, "Son, have you read the Odes?"

"I have not," the boy replied.

"Then read them," Confucius said. "For until you have read them, you are not fit to associate with."[1]

I don't know whether that conversation actually took place, but the story illustrates the key quality of Confucius. He was a man who placed a premium on knowing the wisdom of the past. He was not a very religious person, but he had high moral standards. He attracted many followers who studied his philosophic proverbs and wrote them down for future generations. In fact, the teachings of Confucius were the moral standard for China for more than two thousand years. They still influence the Chinese community on the West Coast of the United States and in other lands.

But we are not so much interested in Confucianism as in what we can learn about paganism by studying the history of Confucianism and its rival Chinese religion, Taoism. How did these pagan religions get started? What was God doing at that time? Why did Confucius and Lao-tsu choose not to worship God? These are the questions we need to answer.

The Man Named Confucius

We know very little about the life of the Chinese philosopher Confucius. His name was actually K'ung Fu-tse, and he was born in the Chinese province of Shantung around 551 B.C. He seems to have come from a poor family and was largely self-educated.

Confucius had a brilliant mind and an insatiable appetite for the wisdom of the past. He studied books of poetry and history, trying to glean the best ideas that wise men had left behind. At age nineteen he secured a government post as an accountant, but he soon grew bored, gave up the job, and opened a school in his home. It is said that he had three thousand students by the time he reached age thirty-four.

Even then he showed evidences of the emphasis which would appear in his wider teachings that were to come later, for while giving instruction in history, poetry, literature, the proprieties, music, natural science, and government, he avoided all references to the supernatural. . . .[2]

Confucius was not like most other teachers of his day who built their teaching of politics, science, art, and other subjects around their religion—their understanding of the supernatural. Confucius was only interested in the practical side of life; he wanted to know how things work and how people behave. He thought the supernatural had nothing to do with that, so he put out of his mind all thoughts about the spirit world. That protected him from some of the more ridiculous pagan ideas of his time, but it also made his teaching primarily humanistic. His goal was to become what he called "Man-at-his-best." He weighed everything by human values and planned everything with human ambitions. He once told a student:

> If for one day you achieve self-control and return to the practice of the rites [of courtesy], the world will acknowledge you as Man-at-his-best. The achieving of Manhood-at-its-best must come from you yourself; one does not acquire it from others![3]

His advice sounds much like the hackneyed slogan that some psychologists use: "Every day in every way I'm getting better and better." It's a totally humanistic method of self-improvement. It assumes that every person has within himself all that he needs to be a whole person. There is no room for help from any outside person or power, no room for God.

The biggest problem with this idea is that humanists refuse to see their sins. Confucius would not confess he was a sinful man; he didn't see anything wrong with being proud and ego-centered. He thought this was natural. So he pushed aside any guilt he may have felt and just kept on trying to learn how to climb the ladder of success.

Even when Confucius taught worthwhile values, he had ulterior motives. He told his students to be courteous and gracious, not because they should love other people, but because these attitudes would help them "get ahead" in life. Take a close look at this conversation Confucius had with another student. Notice the selfish motives he had.

(Confucius:) He who in this world can practice five things may indeed be considered Man-at-his-best.

What are they?

Humility, magnanimity, sincerity, diligence, and graciousness. If you are humble, you will not be laughed at. If you are magnanimous, you will attract many to your side. If you are sincere, people will trust you. If you are gracious, you will get along well with your subordinates.[4]

In other words, Confucius taught his students to behave themselves because that's how they could succeed in life. He was the world's first charm-school teacher. Dale Carnegie was an amateur by comparison; Confucius was teaching young men

"How to Win Friends and Influence People" long before Mr. Carnegie ever thought of it.

When Confucius died, his students built shelters near his tomb so they could study his writings and recite what he had taught them. They wrote down his teachings and began to open schools of their own, to spread the good news of how to become "Man-at-his-best." Within a few years, the Chinese government began building temples in honor of Confucius. They held him in such high esteem that they gradually elevated him to the status of a saint. When Mao Tse-Tung took control of China in 1945, the country had more than fifteen hundred temples to Confucius where the Chinese people burned incense and recited the sayings of Confucius day after day, hoping to follow his formula for success. Confucius would have been the last person to want to start a new religion, but the people worshipped his ideas.

Even Confucius realized that there is a world beyond this one, a life beyond the grave. As much as he criticized religion, he sometimes mentioned the "forces of heaven" or the "will of heaven." He believed that these supernatural forces had given him a mission in life. Once a mob attacked him in the city of Kwang, and he barely escaped with his life. He later told his followers, "Heaven has appointed me to teach this doctrine, and until I have done so, what can the people of Kwang do to me?"[5]

I believe God was trying to break through to this man. Even though Confucius was wrapped up in his pursuit of fame and success, God kept nudging him to think about what lay beyond this world. He could ignore the truth, but he couldn't escape it.

Huston Smith of M.I.T has spent several years studying the writings of Confucius and the cult that grew up around him. Dr. Smith says:

> ... Even the most rationalistically trained Confucianist of today will be inclined to say that ... behind the visible and material world is a spiritual power which in some mysterious way has decreed the ordering laws of the universe.[6]

Confucianism supplied a much-needed moral element to the Chinese national character. It taught politeness and civility in a land that had followed the crude customs of its Mongol ancestors for many generations. Confucius was a welcome reformer, but he fell short of the whole truth. He left men without redemption, without eternal life, without a personal relationship to God. Confucius gave his people a noble philosophy, but it had no soul.

Lao-tsu

At the same time Confucius was alive, another philosopher named Lao-tsu was teaching in the Honan province of northern China. Lao-tsu was almost fifty years older than Confucius, and he was the keeper of the royal archive for the Chou emperors. A Chinese legend says that this elderly man met Confucius in 517 B.C. and criticized him for being so proud and ambitious.

Lao-tsu believed that people did not need to observe stately rituals and formal courtesies to be well-respected. He urged his students to "be themselves." He told each one to find out what sort of person he really was and then act naturally, no matter what other people said. His methods took a 180-degree turn from those of Confucius, but he also believed that a person could make himself happy.

It is said that when Lao-tsu was leaving the city of Honan for the last time, the gatekeeper asked, "How's the road?" Lao-tsu realized that the man had summed up what all of his students wanted to know: How is the road (*tao*) of life? So he sat down and recorded his thoughts in a little book he entitled *Tao teh-King* ("Book of the Virtuous Road"). This book became the core of a new philosophy called Taoism.

The *Tao teh-King* recommended a life of enjoyment and passiveness that allowed other people to "do their own thing." The philosopher summed up his ideas in two lines:

> Appear in plainness and hold to simplicity;
> Restrain selfishness and curtail desires.[7]

Lao-tsu envisioned a world where no one would fight or steal or hate his brother, because everyone would "live and let live." He wanted his followers to find complete harmony with nature and their fellow men.

Naturally, each new generation added some new thoughts to Lao-tsu's ideas. Taoists began to use the magic charms and superstitious rituals that their pagan ancestors had used, and they wove these ideas into Lao-tsu's philosophy. During the first century A.D., the time of Jesus, a Taoist leader named Chang Tao-lin traveled across much of China, using magic rituals to heal people. He taught the people to use secret charms and potions to ward off evil spirits. Before long, Taoism took on all the appearances of an animistic, pagan religion.

Today, Taoism focuses a great deal of attention on the supernatural. It uses sorcery and divination to try to make evil spirits do what the worshipper wants. Taoists consult fortune-tellers, palm readers, tea-leaf readers, and all kinds of wizards who are supposed to foretell the future. Taoism courts the favor of demons and satanic forces, wherever they are found.

A friend of mine watched a group of Taoist priests in a frenzied dance, obviously under the influence of demonic spirits. One of the priests took a sword and twisted it with bare hands until it looked like a corkscrew. When their dance ended, the priest returned to his normal state and was amazed at what he had done. The other priests praised him. One said, "You must be a god if you are able to do this."

Taoists give themselves over to deep meditation, expecting to obtain strength from evil spirits as well as good spirits. It is pathetic to see people so enslaved by the power of Satan. I have been to Tibet and the other border countries of China, and I have seen the wretched condition of these people.

Where Was God?

We ought to ask, "What was God doing during the time of Confucius and Lao-tsu?" Did they have a chance to know the truth?

While these two men were alive, God was sending great prophets like Ezekiel to warn His people of their sins. You will remember that after Solomon's death the Jewish nation divided in two, the northern kingdom being called Israel and the southern kingdom Judah. Israel fell to the Assyrians in 721 B.C. After many years of struggle, Judah fell to the Babylonians in 586 B.C. During the long span of time while Judah stood alone, God sent His messengers to warn its people to repent. In spite of the pagan decadence that pervaded that nation, God was able to raise up men who spoke out for the truth. As the Bible says, "God . . . spoke in time past unto the fathers by the prophets" (Heb. 1:1).

The prophets were not superhuman; they didn't wear halos; they didn't descend from the clouds. They were average, imperfect people. But they stood out from the crowd for one reason: They went after the truth and told it to the world when they found it.

Supposedly, that's what Confucius and Lao-tsu did. They searched for the truth about life, and when they thought they had found it, they began teaching others. But the "truth" they taught was radically different from the truth of God.

Were they mistaken? Perhaps. The conscience of

man can be so corrupted that it can't tell the difference between the truth and a lie (1 Tim. 4:2). This may be what happened to them.

Were they lying? This is another possibility. The world is full of people trying to pass themselves off as saviors of men, though they know they are lying (Mark 13:22). We can't exclude this possibility.

Did God leave them ignorant of Himself? We can be sure this wasn't so. God's Word says He was revealing Himself to them. Isaiah understood God's ability to have His will fulfilled throughout the earth when he wrote:

> The Lord of hosts hath sworn, saying, Surely as I have thought, so shall it come to pass; and as I have purposed, so shall it stand. . . . This is the purpose that is purposed *upon the whole earth:* and this is the hand that is stretched out *upon all the nations* (Is. 14:24,26, italics mine).

God expected all people to obey Him, just as plants and animals obey His laws of nature (Is. 61:11). It should have been a natural response of men and women to the One who had created them. Even if God did not reveal Himself in visions or oracles or prophetic signs, He revealed Himself through all of His blessings (Acts 14:15–17). Yet the wise men of China were not wise enough to worship Him.

Humanism in America

Humanism may have been promoted by Confucius and Lao-tsu, but it certainly didn't stay in

China. The Western world is caught up in a humanistic life-style that lifts the ideals of these Oriental philosophers to a new high. But we are reaping pitiful results, and our troubles have only begun.

A person who looks inside himself for the answers to life's problems will not find answers—just more problems! The human soul is corrupt, carnal, and selfish. It squirms against the idea of discipline; it turns away from suffering. Yet discipline and suffering often lead to a full surrender to Christ, and that is where happiness begins. When you plan your life around your own ambitions or desires, you cut yourself off from other people, except to the extent that they can further your designs! This is humanism, the worship of the human self. It is as pagan as the most ungodly cults of the ancient idol worshippers.

Television commercials reflect the humanism of our society. They say: "It's expensive, but you're worth it"; "Give yourself the best"; and "You deserve a break today." Best-selling books make the message more explicit: *Looking Out for Number One; Be Your Own Boss;* and *Nice Guys Finish Last.* Everything about our modern life-style caters to self-indulgence and selfish ambition. More than ever before, our standards seem to say that man is the center of all things.

Americans have marched in the streets for all kinds of rights—minority rights, women's rights, students' rights, union rights, and so on. But the most important right of all is *birthright*—the privilege of knowing that you are a child of God. The privilege to do whatever you please can bring a sense of thrill and victory, but it does not bring happiness. Why? Because nothing that we can do, nothing that we can be, will make us happy; only what Christ can do for us will make us happy. We don't find the key to happiness by giving ourselves more latitude; we find it by giving Him more. As Peter Marshall says,

> . . . If you let Him take control of your life completely, if you are willing to bow to His will for you, then you will enter into that transforming fellowship which brings with it that glorious exhilaration, that indescribable peace, and escape from all bondage. . . .[8]

Exhilaration . . . peace . . . escape . . . these are the things the Chinese philosophers looked for. But they looked in the wrong place.

Where are you looking?

11

ISLAM:
Worshipping the Wrong God

In the past few chapters, we have been dealing with a question that has bothered me for a long time: "Where was God when pagan religions began?" We have seen that several pagan religions emerged at the same time God was establishing His covenant with Israel. The leaders of these pagan cults chose to turn away from God, even when they saw God's power demonstrated in the Hebrew people. We have found plenty of biblical evidence that God was trying to communicate with all people in all nations, because He loved them all. But powerful nations like Egypt, Babylonia, and China insisted on making their own gods rather than worshipping the one true God.

Now we are going to skip ahead in history to look at a very unusual pagan religion. It is the only major pagan religion to be founded *after* the time of Christ. In fact, it was founded long after the New Testament had been written, when copies of the Word were easily available. We are sure the founder had heard the gospel of Jesus Christ, because he married a Christian woman and often mentioned Jesus in his writings. Yet this man insisted Jesus was not the

Son of God, and he went on to start another pagan religion. Today, his religion has about 455 million followers. It is one of the most influential religions of the modern world.

I am talking about the religion of Islam. This is the predominant religion of Egypt, Iran, Afghanistan, and so many other nations in the news today. It is a religion that Christians should know more about.

When Islam Was Born

Islam had its beginnings with a man named Mohammed. He was born in the caravan town of Mecca on the sands of the Arabian Desert in about A.D. 570. Both of his parents died shortly after Mohammed was born, so he was raised by his grandfather and uncle. He spent his teen-age years herding sheep and leading camel caravans across the desert.

Mohammed's life took a hopeful turn at age twenty-four when he married Khadija, a wealthy woman who had employed him for caravan work. With this newly gained wealth, Mohammed left the caravan trade and spent most of his time in meditation.

At the age of forty, Mohammed was meditating in a cave of Mount Hira, near Mecca, when he had a vision calling him to preach. He returned to town and proclaimed himself *Ali* (Arabic, "the divine prophet"). His wife became his first convert.

A few months later, Mohammed's wife died, and he married two other women—one a Jewess and the other a Christian. We can be sure that these women introduced him to the Scriptures of the Old and New Testament. Yet Mohammed kept on preaching about a different God from the One revealed in Scripture. He declared that the only god was named Allah, and that Allah was a stern, vindictive god whose followers had to follow strict rituals to please him.

Mohammed was a very strong leader who believed he should use military force to make other people accept his new religion. He gathered a band of caravan thieves and roustabouts who pledged their loyalty to him in return for "a piece of the action" when he gained control of Mecca. But the Jews and Christians of Mecca resisted the pagan prophet's methods, and an angry mob tried to kill him in 622. He fled to the city of Yathrib, which he later renamed Medina. His followers later called his escape the *Hegira* (Arabic, "flight"), and they believe it marked the beginning of their Islamic religion.

Mohammed and his men soon took control of Yathrib and made it the center of their religion. They built up an army of vagabonds to raid nearby camps; they told Christians and Jews living in Yathrib that they could either accept Mohammed's beliefs or pack their bags and leave.

Mohammed became the absolute ruler of Yathrib, where he founded his model theocratic state. He built the first mosque [Islamic house of worship],

changed the direction of prayers from Jerusalem to
Mecca, and instituted the fast month of Ramadan
and tithing. Relations with Christians and Jews de-
teriorated, but eventually he made treaties granting
them freedom of worship in return for taxes.[1]

Mohammed enforced strict discipline in the city.
He required his followers to pray, bowing toward
his hometown of Mecca. He allowed no one to drink
wine. He ordered everyone to fast during the day-
light hours in the month of Ramadan. And he
exacted a tithe from everyone, in order to support
his religio-political empire.

Mohammed liked to absorb the best from other
religions he encountered. He mentioned Abraham
and the other patriarchs in the Koran, along with
Jesus, Mary, and several others from the New Testament, asserting that all of these people were servants of Allah. Moreover, he listed ninety-nine
names of Allah in the Koran; apparently, they were
names he had picked up from other pagan religions.
To this day, Muslims count prayer rosaries with
ninety-nine beads—each bead representing a name
of Allah.

The Five Pillars

For twenty years, Mohammed ruled Medina and
perfected his system of government. He compiled
all of his ideas in a book called the *Koran* (Arabic,
"reading"), which Muslims believe was inspired by

Allah. The Koran spells out the basic principles of the Islamic faith, which are known as "Five Pillars of Islam":

1. *Recitation of the Kalima.* A Muslim is required to say this creed over and over again in public to let others know about his faith. The Kalima creed says: "There is no god but Allah, and Mohammed is the Prophet of Allah."

2. *Prayer five times daily.* The Koran requires Muslims to pray only three times a day, but later Muslim leaders changed this to five times—dawn, noon, afternoon, evening, and night. A man called a *muezzin* climbs to the top of a high tower on the Muslim mosque to announce each time of prayer. Muslims still must bow toward Mecca when they pray.

3. *Almsgiving.* The Koran does not require any certain percentage of a person's giving, but it says that a person must give a portion of his income to help the poor and sick.

4. *Fasting in the month of Ramadan.* This is the most holy month of the Islamic calendar. Muslims must follow very harsh regulations during this month (which lasts about six weeks, since it is figured on a lunar calendar).

> During the daylight hours [of Ramadan] the Muslim must not swallow even his spittle, and must abstain from sexual enjoyment. The night is not mentioned, so the faithful eat and drink at night, and the less orthodox even indulge themselves after dusk.[2]

5. *Pilgrimage to Mecca*. At least once during his lifetime, every Muslim must visit Mohammed's hometown of Mecca during the last month of the Islamic year. If a person is unable to go, he may pay someone to go in his place. (Many poor Muslims visit Mecca each year as proxies of wealthier Muslims, who would rather not leave home!)

The Koran also describes a sixth "pillar," the *Jihad,* or holy war. Mohammed urged his followers to fight on behalf of Allah, expanding the domain of Islam to other nations. However, Jihad has not been mandatory in modern times.[3]

Wars of Expansion

Mohammed and his immediate successors used *Jihad* to seize many Christian territories of the old Roman Empire. By the time Mohammed died in A.D. 632, Islam held control of the entire Arabian Peninsula. The next leaders of Islam (the *caliphs*) marched through Palestine and spread across northern Africa to the region where Algeria is today. They crossed the Strait of Gibralter in A.D. 711 and began conquering the Christian cities of Spain and France. Their zeal for Allah gave them a passion to conquer the world. But Charles Martel (grandfather of Charlemagne) defeated the Muslim armies in a bloody battle at Tours in central France, driving them back to the Pyrenees Mountains. This was surely a miracle of God, because Charles' forces were fewer and less inexperienced than the Muslims'. Had he not stopped the Islamic armies, they might have blotted out Christianity in western Europe, and America might have been an Islamic nation.

Defeated in the west, Islam pushed eastward into central Asia. Irresistibly, century by century, Islam made converts until most of northern India had fallen under the Muslim sword. Then Islam moved into the Far East, overrunning Java and several islands of the South Pacific, including the Philippines. In the Philippines today, the Muslims (called Moros) comprise the most powerful cultural minority of the nation. They live primarily on the southern islands of Mindanao, where they pose a constant challenge to the Christians living on other Filipino islands.

At the height of their power, the Muslim states occupied more territory than the Roman Empire ever did. One can find evidence of the Islamic conquests throughout Spain, northern Africa, and central Asia. For example, Islam is still the state religion of nations such as Mauritania (western Africa), Iran (Middle East), and Malaysia (Southeast Asia). Muslim mosques can still be found in Spain, Lebanon, and other countries that fell to the Muslims' holy wars.

It is astonishing to see the power of the Islamic religion today. The governments of many Islamic countries feel pressure from their religious leaders, who want Islam to take charge of government affairs. This has already happened in Iran where the Ayatollah Khomeini and other Islamic holy men "call the shots" in government. Nearly every day, our newspapers and television news reports tell of political trouble being stirred up by the Muslim religious leaders, who keep these countries in constant turmoil.

In most countries where Islam is the state religion, the laws guarantee freedom of religion. But anyone who visits these countries soon discovers that the Muslim leaders are ready to use force to make the people stand fast in the Islamic faith. There is real persecution in some lands where the Islamic faith is very strong.

One Muslim was asked, "Do you believe in freedom of religion?"

"Of course I do," he replied. "All Muslims believe in freedom of religion."

"Then what if your son became a Christian? What would you do?"

"I'd cut his throat," the Muslim said.

We need to pray for the people who live in such circumstances, pray that God will awaken them to the truth.

Mohammed called Christians "the idolaters," because the church of his day had fallen into corruption and was devoted to images and statues of the saints. Many Christians converted to Islam, hoping to find something better. Mohammed said of the Christians he met:

> When they listen to that which hath been revealed unto the messenger [i.e., Mohammed], thou seest their eyes overflow with tears because of their rec-

ognition of the Truth. They say: Our Lord, we believe. Inscribe us as among the witnesses.[4]

This surely must have happened, because hundreds of thousands of Christians converted to Islam,
many of them because they feared the Muslim war-
riors. Many others defected, however, because the
church of their day was spiritually dead. This ought
to be a warning to us Christians today.

Where Was God?
Where was God when the pagan religion of Islam
was born? Despite the corruption that dominated
much of the church, God was still very active in the
world. The Muslims could see what He was doing;
they saw plenty of evidence that Christians were
following the true God.

Saint Patrick preached the gospel in Ireland about
one hundred years before Mohammed was born. He
established some strong churches on the Emerald
Isle, and these churches produced fiery evangelists
who carried the gospel back to the continent of
Europe. (Most Europeans were still observing the
pagan superstitions of their barbaric ancestors.)
About the time Mohammed was driving the camels
across the desert, an Irish monk named Columbanus
traveled across what is now France and Germany,
winning thousands of people to Christ. In England,
Christian monks established great libraries where
they could study and copy the Word of God. All of
these efforts strengthened the church in western

Europe—one reason why the Europeans decided to fight the Muslims when they charged northward out of Spain.

But God was also at work in Mohammed's life. God brought him into contact with several Christian people; Mecca itself was a Christian city. Mohammed heard the gospel of Jesus Christ from the lips of people who had accepted Him as their Savior. Yet he twisted the gospel to suit his own outlandish ideas. Dr. John Alden Williams, a lecturer at the Institute of Islamic Studies at McGill University, summarizes what the Koran says about Jesus.

> Jesus holds a unique place among the prophets in Islam. He is born of a virgin "purified above all women," he is the promised Messiah, "The Word of God and a Spirit from Him," an almost superhuman figure who spoke from the cradle and worked great wonders by the power of God; but the central doctrines of Christianity are set aside. The idea that he is the Son of God is sternly rejected, the doctrine of the Trinity is held to contradict God's Oneness. . . . The early Christians are held to have deliberately falsified the scripture he brought, and to have worshiped the Messiah blasphemously. Later generations have been perhaps sincere but certainly misguided, so that a new revelation became necessary. As for Jesus, God took him to Himself when the Jews rejected him [without Jesus' being crucified], and will justify him before the end of the world.[5]

Some people believe that Islam is quite similar to Christianity or Judaism, but nothing could be farther from the truth. Muslims worship one god and we worship one God, but there all similarity ends. Mohammed's "god" is radically different from God as He is revealed to us by the Bible. Mohammed's god is a spiteful, selfish autocrat who must be placated with a monotonous routine of holy motions. The God we worship is a loving, compassionate Father who asks only that we love Him in return. The late missionary Robert H. Glover observed that the god of Islam, "far from being the loving and beneficent God of the Christian Bible, is an unfeeling despot, infinitely removed from His creatures, with no mediator between."[6]

This is the tragic error of Mohammed's religion. He was right to realize there is only one God; but he was dead wrong to think that God must be like a human ruler, having superhuman powers. God is holy, while man is sinful. This is why we need Jesus to act as our Mediator—not because God is so vain that He doesn't want to communicate with us, but because we are so sinful that we need someone to remove our sins from His sight. Muslims are proud people who feel they earn Allah's blessings with their prayers and rituals. But we Christians know we do not deserve God's goodness and never could deserve it. God blesses us because He loves us.

It is just as pagan to worship the wrong god as it is to worship no god, or to worship a whole pantheon of gods.

I am shocked to think the religion of Islam has drawn so many millions of people away from God.

This should shake us up. It should make us realize that we have a duty to preach the gospel and expose the teachings of paganism for what they really are. It should cause us to pray that God will keep on revealing Himself to the Muslim community. I earnestly hope that our Muslim neighbors will turn back to Him before it's too late.

12

END-TIME PAGANISM

You might think that paganism would be weakening by now. With evangelists and missionaries spreading the gospel around the globe, it seems that pagan ideas would be gradually snuffed out. But just the opposite is true. Paganism is stronger than ever and is growing faster than the world's population. Each year Christians are a smaller and smaller minority in the world.

In our country, all kinds of heretical cults, the occult, and psychic research are leading people away from God. Americans want to find a power beyond themselves to cope with their problems, and Satan has been only too happy to oblige. He is supplying all kinds of ungodly, paganistic ideas to divert people from God.

For example, I understand that the Soviet Union spends fifty million dollars each year on psychic research. They hope to find a way to read and/or control other people's minds. This would be an important military discovery, of course. Fortune tellers do a thriving business in most of our cities. Our young people experiment with ouija boards and seances, because they are curious about the spirit world. These things are paganistic.

Jesus predicted that this would happen. He said that paganism would gain more influence just before He returned. I believe we are entering the end-times. Let me share a few Scriptures that indicate this is so.

The Antichrist and False Prophets

Second Thessalonians 2:7–12 suggests that the last world ruler will be both a political and religious ruler. This "lawless one" will be deceitful, and he will lead most of the world into unrighteousness and paganism. Everyone who follows him, everyone who is ready to be deceived by him, will be condemned to die when Christ returns. A person must want to know the truth in order to be saved.

Jesus predicted that false prophets will come and claim to be messengers of God; some will even claim to be Christ (Matt. 24:5). But Jesus warned, "Take heed that no man deceive you" (Matt. 24:4). People can be so gullible that they will believe anything, even a cult leader who claims to be Christ. We need to be very careful about who we follow. We should examine in the light of God's Word what our leaders teach, to be sure they are being faithful to the truth. As John said, we should "try the spirits whether they are of God" (1 John 4:1).

Paul predicted that many people will fall away from Christ and follow after these false prophets. He wrote to Timothy,

> Now the Spirit expressly says that in latter times some will depart from the faith by giving heed to deceitful spirits and doctrines of demons . . . (1 Tim. 4:1 NKJV–NT).

We can see this happening all around us today. Thousands of Christians are getting so lax in Bible study and prayer, and their relationship with Christ is growing so cold, that it is easy for them to be pulled aside by pagan and heretical cults. They are letting their defenses down. They are "giving heed" to the lies of Satan. They are backsliding from their Christian faith.

Yet the Bible encourages us to wait patiently for the coming of the Lord, which will come like the "latter rain" that gave an abundant harvest to the people of Israel (James 5:7). J. Barton Payne notes that the "latter rain" is a prophetic symbol of "prosperity and abundance . . . in the millennial kingdom" of Christ (cf. Ps. 72:6).[1] This is not just an abundance of material things, but an abundance of spiritual things as well. Just before Christ returns, God will pour out a new "shower" of His grace upon the earth.

I believe this is happening right now. We are seeing miracles such as Jesus performed when He walked the streets of Jerusalem nineteen hundred years ago. I am delighted to hear the reports of a great revival among Catholic and Lutheran people; in nearly all of the mainline denominational

145

churches, there is a new surge of repentance and faithfulness to God. This could be the "latter rain" of God's grace. The Bible tells us to put our faith and trust in God and to wait patiently for Jesus to come back. No matter how powerful the forces of paganism become, we can expect great blessing from God just before the end. As all of these things happen, we can be sure that the Lord's return is drawing near.

When Jesus Comes

Why don't you open your Bible to 1 Thessalonians 5 and read what Paul had to say about Jesus' second coming. He predicted that Jesus will seem to come like "a thief in the night" (v. 2); the world will be so wrapped up in its sin that it won't notice His coming. The pagan rulers of the world will tell everyone that things are going just fine; "peace and safety" will be their motto (v. 3). But at that very time, God's Son will come to judge them.

Paul says there are two kinds of people in the world today: people of light and people of darkness (vv. 4,5). If you follow Jesus Christ, you belong to the Light; if you don't, you belong to the darkness. The people of darkness will be overwhelmed by their own lies, but the people of light will shine brighter and brighter—they will grow more and more faithful to Christ—until the day He returns.

Many people are walking after their own lusts, their own opinions, and their own wickedness. I think of Jim Jones and his cult called the Peoples'

Temple. Jones started out by quoting the Bible, but he finally laid the Bible aside and told his followers they ought to build a Communist-style society. Eventually, he made them commit suicide with him. This is a prime example of the pagan ideas that are becoming more widespread these days. It's a sign that Christ could return at any time.

God is long-suffering and merciful. He does not want anyone to perish, not even the most rebellious pagan. Remember the verse that we noted earlier:

> The Lord is not slack concerning His promise, . . . but is longsuffering to us-ward, not willing that any should perish, but that all should come to repentance (2 Pet. 3:9).

This is one of the Bible's most wonderful promises for the unbeliever. It means that everyone has a chance to accept Christ before He returns. Everyone can receive God's gift of eternal life, offered through the Savior. This is the most thrilling news the world has ever heard.

But the apostle Peter didn't stop there. He went on to describe the day when Christ will return. It's not a pretty picture, because Christ will return to find a world engulfed in paganism, and He will deal with it accordingly.

> . . . The heavens shall pass away with a great noise, and the elements shall melt with fervent heat, the earth also and the works that are therein shall be burned up. . . .

Ye therefore, beloved, seeing ye know these things before, beware lest ye also, being led away with the error of the wicked, fall from your own stedfastness. (2 Pet. 3:10,17).

What a sobering statement! It makes us realize how serious this business of paganism is. We can expect pagan religions to deceive and win more people every year until the Lord returns. We must do everything we can to make these ungodly people realize the price they will have to pay, and we must be careful not to slip into paganism ourselves.

13

THE RISE
OF CHRISTIANITY

And he said unto them, Go ye into all the world, and preach the gospel to every creature. He that believeth and is baptized shall be saved; but he that believeth not shall be damned (Mark 16:15,16).

With these words, Jesus sent His disciples out into the world to spread the good news of His resurrection. This Great Commission became the commission of all Christians; it became the rallying point for Jesus' followers. They plunged into the world of the first century—and it was largely a pagan world—to call men and women back to God. They faced all kinds of persecution, but the orders of their Lord kept them moving.

I want us to think about the early Christians' answer to paganism, because it will show us how we ought to respond to it today. No one can doubt that we live in a very secularized world, where everything is geared toward the greedy glorification of self; we live in a pagan world. We Christians had better learn from the apostles how to respond to this world, before it strips away our faith.

We can begin by looking at how they understood

the Great Commission that I just quoted. What did it mean to them? How did it affect their lives after Jesus returned to heaven? And how should it affect our lives today, as we like the apostles face so many pagan religions?

The Lord's Authority

The apostles received the Great Commission as their top-priority instructions because Jesus was the top-priority leader in their lives. They knew that the Old Testament prophets had predicted Jesus would come. Isaiah had said:

> . . . The government shall be upon his shoulder: and his name shall be called Wonderful, Counsellor, The mighty God, The everlasting Father, The Prince of Peace. Of the increase of his government and peace there shall be no end . . . (Is. 9:6,7).

Isaiah, Jeremiah, Ezekiel, and other prophets foretold that Christ would change the whole world when He came. Nations outside Israel would receive the truth and give their allegiance to the Lord (Hag. 2:7; Zech. 2:11). Christ would belong to the entire world. Everyone who believed in Him would be saved; no one who came to Him would be rejected.

The apostles knew these prophecies had been fulfilled when Jesus came to earth. He walked among the downtrodden of humanity—born in a stable, raised in a carpenter's shop, executed on a cross between two thieves. Yet Jesus blessed everyone in

150

His path; He healed everyone who asked to be healed and forgave the sins of everyone who asked His forgiveness. When He went to die on Calvary, He paid the supreme price of love for all mankind. He became the sacrificial Lamb of God who took away the sin of the *world*—all the world (John 1:29). There on the cross He became the Sin-Bearer of all mankind in all generations. Rising from the dead, He became the Lord of all (1 Cor. 15:20,21,25,26).

Jesus Christ completely fulfilled the design of the heavenly Father for the redemption of the human race. He fulfilled *all* of it! He paid the total price for human rebellion against God, including the rebellion of every pagan religion devised by man. He revealed the unconquerable love of God, reaching out to the descendants of Adam, the descendants of Noah, the dispersed tribes of Babel, and the peoples of all the broken continents. Satan scattered people and pitted neighbor against neighbor; but Christ reconciled people with one another, because He died for all of them on the cross. The disciples knew this. They knew He was the long-promised Son of God, so they were eager to take their marching orders from Him.

Jesus sent them into the world with a message of saving truth, as the early results of their ministry proved. People's lives were dramatically changed when they accepted Jesus as their Savior and Lord. "Ye shall receive power," Jesus promised His disciples (Acts 1:8); the marvelous things that happened under their ministry confirmed that the Holy Spirit indeed gave them power. Three thousand

151

people gave their lives to Christ when Peter preached the first Christian sermon in Jerusalem (Acts 2:41). Every day, more people accepted the good news of Christ and surrendered themselves to Him (Acts 2:47). Soon the apostles were scattered throughout the known world, carrying with them the message of salvation. Christ had told them, "Go into all the world," so they did not intend to leave any part of the world untouched.

The Disciples and Their Work

Who were these men who made Christianity a world religion? They were not great intellectuals or mystics. They were common, ordinary men— fishermen, tax collectors, tent makers, and so on. Yet they had been privileged to sit with Jesus. He said,

> . . . Many prophets and righteous men have desired to see those things which ye see, and have not seen them; and to hear those things which ye hear, and have not heard them (Matt. 13:17).

They certainly were fortunate. Christ had chosen them to be the foundation stone of His glorious church. They took up their task with real devotion, forsaking everything else to serve Jesus. Not everyone was willing to do this; more than one man refused because of the hardships involved (Matt. 8:19–22). But the courageous men who did follow Jesus had a life more exciting and rewarding than they ever could have dreamed.

Andrew was one of the first disciples Jesus chose. He was a fisherman by trade, a very compassionate man. When Andrew left Jerusalem, he carried the gospel to the area of the Black Sea (now southern Russia), Asia Minor, and Greece. Tradition says that when he was crucified in Achaia (now southern Greece), he hung on his cross for two days, begging bystanders to give their hearts to Jesus.

Simon Peter was Andrew's brother, and perhaps the best-known of the apostles. He went to strengthen the church in Rome, a city so wicked that he called it "Babylon" (1 Pet. 5:13). Peter was a very impetuous man, apt to speak before thinking what might happen. He established the precedent of receiving Gentiles into the church, because he knew that Christ came to save all nationalities. We are told that the Emperor Nero had Peter crucified in the garden of his palace, but the apostle insisted on being hung head-down because he felt unworthy to die like Jesus.

John was called "the beloved disciple" because he loved Jesus so much and had such a gentle disposition. Helen Kooiman Hosier says,

> No one knew Jesus better than John, yet one senses from his writing that he was a very modest man . . . [He was] the poet, the dreamer, the mystic, the seer. . . .[1]

As He hung on the cross, Jesus entrusted His own mother into John's care. This indicates the deep love and confidence that Jesus had for John. When

John and his brother James first came to Jesus, they were so ambitious and outspoken that Jesus called them "sons of thunder" (Mark 3:17; cf. Mark 10:35–40). But John matured under Jesus' guidance. In later years, the Roman government exiled John to the Isle of Patmos, where he had the colossal vision of Christ's return that he recorded in the Book of Revelation. He returned to his home in Ephesus just before he died.

James, the brother of John, was one of the three intimate friends of Jesus (along with John and Peter). He was present at the Transfiguration and during Jesus' agony in the Garden of Gethsemane—the most glorious and the most humbling experiences of Jesus' ministry. So he knew Jesus very well, and he acclaimed Him as his Lord. James became the leader of the church in Jerusalem and was beheaded by King Herod in about A.D. 44 (Acts 12:1,2).

Philip was one of the first disciples that Jesus called. He seldom appears in the Gospels, and when he does, he always seems to be assisting one of the other apostles. We might say he was the "helper" in the group. (He should not be confused with Philip the evangelist mentioned in Acts.) Tradition says that the apostle Philip went to preach at Hieropolis, where most of the citizens followed a pagan serpent cult. Many people accepted Christ under Philip's preaching, but his enemies captured him and hanged him on a pillar along one of the city streets.

Matthew was a tax collector under contract to the Roman government. The Jews despised him because he levied the hated Roman fees, yet Jesus stopped by his tax table one day and simply said "Follow me," and Matthew got up and followed Him (Luke 5:27,28). Being a tax collector, Matthew undoubtedly was a well-educated man; he probably knew Greek, Aramaic, and Latin.[2] He was well-qualified to write an account of Jesus' life. Matthew apparently became a missionary to the Persians; legend says that he was martyred in Ethiopia.

Bartholomew, a disciple scarcely mentioned in the New Testament, is said to have become a missionary to Armenia, where he was executed by whip-lashing. Another tradition says that he went to India.[3]

Thomas was the disciple who doubted that Jesus had risen from the dead until the Savior let him touch His wounds (John 20:24–28). From that moment, Thomas became an evangelist of great faith and courage. Historians have found several documents that indicate Thomas preached the gospel in the city of Edessa, in eastern Syria.[4] Eusebius reported that Thomas went to India and died a martyr's death near Madras.

James the Less, also known as James the Younger, is thought to have written the Epistle of James. He recorded God's advice to be patient during the troubles that Christians would experience before the Lord's return (James 5:7,8); no doubt he experienced many of those troubles firsthand. Tradition tells us that James was crucified in Egypt, where he had gone to preach.

Thaddeus, also called "Judas not Iscariot" or "Jude," took the gospel message to the nations of Mesopotamia. Thaddeus is quietly in the background as we read about Jesus' life, but he wrote an inspiring New Testament epistle that bears his name; and he won untold numbers of pagan worshippers to Christ. We are told that he was martyred in Persia.

Simon Zelotes, or Simon the Zealot, is another disciple who escapes the limelight of the gospel writers' narratives. But we can be sure that he learned much from Jesus during the brief years of his discipleship. Eusebius and other early Christian writers say that Simon succeeded James as head of the church in Jerusalem.[5]

So it appears that the apostles went into every major region of the known world. They declared the good news of Jesus Christ and established the church in every pagan culture they encountered. They were willing to sacrifice everything they had, even their lives, to tell the world about the Lord.

Of course, martyrdom did not stop with them. Many of the early church fathers gave their life's blood for the gospel, dying in Roman sports arenas, in public squares, and in rat-infested dungeons throughout the Roman Empire and in the barbaric lands beyond.

If we study martyrdom under Hadrian and Marcus Aurelius, we find that the most notable of these martyrs suffered at pagan festivals. This is true of

Polycarp, martyred in Smyrna on the occasion of the festival given by the Asiarch Philip [A.D. 169], and of the martyrs of Lyons in 177, thrown to wild animals during the festival which every year brought [pagan] delegates from the three Gauls together at Lyons.

. . . Surprise has sometimes been shown that under liberal, philosophical emperors like the Antonines there were martyrs, but the fact is that under the humanist veneer Graeco-Roman civilization still had a core of cruelty.[6]

The church has always been forced to pay a price for carrying out its mission. The cruel, diabolical agents of pagan religions have often exacted this price in human blood. Thousands of young converts have deserted Christ because they didn't want to sacrifice themselves to be faithful. But enough have stayed to carry the gospel to every continent and every generation since the time of Christ; millions of souls have been saved. The apostles still give us a worthy example to follow.

Christianity and the World

Christians have the most important message in the world. We should work together to send that message to every person alive; we should give everyone a challenge to accept Christ as their Savior before He returns to establish His kingdom. Jesus said, "The gospel must first be preached to all the nations" before He will return (Mark 13:10). Even though pagans have had opportunity after opportunity to serve the living God, they must be confronted with the truth one last time before Jesus comes back.

Christianity is not just another religion among all the religions that compete for man's attention. It is *the* religion. It is the religion that fulfills God's eternal plan to bring mankind back into fellowship with Him. In a very real sense, Christianity began in the Garden of Eden when God promised to send a Savior, a descendant of Eve, who would defeat the power of Satan (Gen. 3:15). Men have tried to construct their own ways back to God, much as the builders of Babel tried to make a stairway to heaven. But God's way, through His Son, Jesus Christ, is still the only way. Anyone who ignores the way is sure to be lost.

How well I remember pacing the deck of a large oceanliner on a sea voyage one night, talking with the captain of the ship. I finally asked, "Captain, what do you think of Jesus? Do you believe He is God in the flesh, God among men?"

The captain paused for a moment. Then he looked up and said, "Mr. Sumrall, those stars are my gods."

I turned the captain back from the rail and stared him straight in the eye. "Captain," I said, "my God made your gods."

We Christians need to be more forthright in telling others about Jesus. We need to "lay it on the line." No one does a greater disservice to God than a Christian who's shy about the gospel.

Three generations of Charles W. Forman's family have been missionaries to China, so he knows what it's like to live in a pagan culture and minister on behalf of Christ. Dr. Forman points out that there's no room for other religions in God's plan. Jesus' death on Calvary provides everything that's necessary for men and women to find their way back to God.

> They no longer need worry about fulfilling the ancient laws conveyed by Moses in order to be acceptable to God—or the later laws conveyed by Mohammed. They need not follow the Hindu paths of divine knowledge, good deeds, or devotion, nor master the exercise of yoga in order to be one with God. The eightfold path of Buddhism is no longer necessary. Sacrifices are useless. What remains is this: *God has done what is necessary to overcome the separation, and men need only recognize and rejoice in what God has done.*[7]

Isn't that wonderful? Don't you feel a burden lifted off your shoulders every time you think about it? We are no longer slaves to superstition, magic, or rituals; we don't depend on any of these things to give us peace with God. Jesus has already restored our bond with God. Hallelujah!

A Privilege—and a Duty

As we've looked at each of the leading pagan religions of our world, we've asked, "Where was God when these pagan religions began?" The answer is obvious: He was there all the time. No matter where or how a pagan religion began, God was there trying to reveal Himself to the founders and followers of the pagan cult. They were not ignorant of God. They simply chose not to follow Him. When Christ returns to judge the world, they will stand to account for that decision, and they will be sentenced to die in hell with the rest of Satan's army.

We Christians are privileged people. We are privileged to know the truth through Jesus Christ. But that makes us responsible for telling others about Him. This isn't easy to do; in fact, it may require us to make some sacrifices. But sacrifice is a strategy that Satan can't disarm.

Jesus could not have saved the world by healing the sick, nor by multiplying bread, nor by teaching the crowds. He could save the world only by sacrificing Himself. You and I cannot do it any cheaper.

So many Christians today are reluctant to sacrifice. They give money as long as they have a surplus; they visit the sick as long as they're in the neighborhood; they witness to someone as long as that person asks about Christ. But beyond that, they're afraid to give anything to God's kingdom.

Friend, the church was established because Christ died for it. The church continued because the apostles died for it. And the church today will win the world for Christ only if we're willing to sacrifice—even die—for it. No amount of money will buy people out of paganism; no amount of arguing will persuade them out of paganism. It's the Spirit of Christ within us, controlling us and filling us, that will win them out of paganism.

Wherever paganism is growing, God is there. He's there through the inward witness of His Holy Spirit; He's there through the outward witness of you and me.

May God help us to reach this dying world while there's still time.

NOTES

Chapter 1

1. I don't mean to imply that God was silent in other parts of the world. A careful study of American Indian religions and the religions of Central America, for example, shows that they were strongly monotheistic—i.e., they exalted one god. These religions never grasped the full truth of the Lord God, but it seems that they caught some sense of the truth He was trying to reveal to them.

2. Louis Berkhof, *Systematic Theology* (Grand Rapids, William B. Eerdmans, 1941), p. 295.

3. The court records of Egypt were very complete, so the pharaoh was not ignorant of what God had done through Abraham and Joseph. Their names were surely recorded in the annals of Egyptian royal history, so the pharaoh must have known how the God of Abraham, Isaac, and Jacob had manifested His power. But Pharaoh wanted gods that he could worship as he pleased.

4. Emile Durkheim, *The Elementary Forms of the Religious Life*, trans. Joseph Ward Swain (New York: The Free Press, 1965), pp. 162–63.

5. Nebuchadnezzar had seen God deliver three men from a fiery furnace (Dan. 3).

Chapter 2

1. Lester Sumrall, *Demons: The Answer Book* (Nashville: Thomas Nelson, 1979), pp. 105–17.

Chapter 3

1. Ralph L. Beals and Harry Hoijer, *An Introduction to Anthropology*, 3rd ed. (New York: Macmillan, 1965), p. 573.

2. Eugene A. Nida, *Customs and Cultures* (New York: Harper and Row, 1954), p. 148.

3. Mark 16:17,18.

Chapter 4

1. Josephus, *Antiquities* 1. 7. 2.

NOTES

2. William Smith, *A Dictionary of the Bible,* ed. by F. N. and M. A. Peloubet (Nashville: Thomas Nelson, 1979), p. 158.

3. Notice that some of the plagues demonstrated the foolishness of Egyptian religion, besides persuading the pharaoh to let the Hebrews go. For example, the Egyptians worshipped frogs, flies, and grasshoppers, so God sent an abundance of each one to afflict them.

4. Ralph Earle, "The Acts of the Apostles," *Beacon Bible Commentary,* vol. 7 (Kansas City: Beacon Hill Press, 1965), pp. 357–58.

Chapter 5

1. Thorkild Jacobsen, "Babel," *The Interpreter's Dictionary of the Bible,* vol. 1 (Nashville: Abingdon Press, 1962), p. 334.

2. William Smith, *A Dictionary of the Bible,* ed. by F. N. and M. A. Peloubet (Nashville: Thomas Nelson, 1979), p. 72.

Chapter 6

1. Pierre Berton, *The Comfortable Pew* (Philadelphia: J. B. Lippincott, 1965), pp. 15–16.

Chapter 7

1. Louis Renou, ed., *Hinduism* (New York: George Braziller, 1962), p. 17.

2. David G. Bradley, *A Guide to the World's Religions* (Englewood Cliffs, N. J.: Prentice-Hall, Inc., 1963), p. 95.

3. Louis Renou, *Hinduism,* p. 54.

4. *The Song of God: Bhagavad-Gita,* trans. by Swami Prabhavananda and Christopher Isherwood (New York: New American Library, 1951), p. 39.

5. Harold R. Cook, *An Introduction to the Study of Christian Missions* (Chicago: Moody Press, 1954), p. 11.

6. *Srimad Bhagavatam: Tenth Canto,* trans. by A. C. Bhaktivedanta Swami Prabhupada (New York: The Bhaktivedanta Book Trust, 1977) p. 312.

Chapter 8

1. E. A. Burtt, ed., *The Teachings of the Compassionate Buddha* (New York: New American Library, 1955), p. 50.

2. H. S. Vigeveno, *The Listener* (Glendale, Calif.: Regal Books, 1971), pp. 128–29.

3. Eugene A. Nida, *Customs and Cultures* (New York: Harper and Row, 1954), p. 261.

4. Richard A. Gard, ed., *Buddhism* (New York: George Braziller, 1961), p. 79.

5. Nida, *Customs and Cultures,* p. 173.

Chapter 9

1. Seymour Kurtz, ed., *The New York Times Encyclopedic Almanac: 1970* (New York: The New York Times, 1970), p. 437.

2. David G. Bradley, *A Guide to the World's Religions* (Englewood Cliffs, N. J.: Prentice-Hall, Inc., 1963), p. 156.

3. Elton Trueblood, *Foundations for Reconstruction*, rev. ed. (Waco, Tex.: Word Books, 1972), p. 20.

Chapter 10

1. Charles S. Braden, *The World's Religions* (Nashville: Abingdon Press, 1954), p. 137.

2. Robert O. Ballou, ed., *The Portable World Bible* (New York: The Viking Press, 1944), p. 486.

3. *The Sayings of Confucius*, trans. by James R. Ware (New York: New American Library, 1955), p. 76.

4. Ibid., p. 110.

5. *The Analects* 9. 5.

6. Huston Smith, *The Religions of Man* (New York: Harper and Row, 1958), p. 191.

7. Robert O. Ballou, *The Portable World Bible*, p. 545.

8. Catherine Marshall, ed., *Mr. Jones, Meet the Master* (Old Tappan, N. J.: Fleming H. Revell, 1966), p. 132.

Chapter 11

1. Seymour Kurtz, ed., *The New York Times Encyclopedic Almanac: 1970* (New York: The New York Times, 1970), p. 436.

2. David G. Bradley, *A Guide to the World's Religions* (Englewood Cliffs, N. J.: Prentice-Hall, Inc., 1963), p. 72.

3. During World War I, Germany tried to get Arab nations to launch a Jihad against the Allied powers, but they refused. More recently, the Palestine Liberation Front has tried to start a Jihad against Israel, without success.

4. Mohammed M. Pickthall, *The Meaning of the Glorious Koran* (New York: New American Library, n.d.), p. 104.

5. John Alden Williams, ed., *Islam* (New York: George Braziller, 1962), pp. 31–32.

6. Robert H. Glover, *The Progress of World-Wide Missions*, rev. by J. Herbert Kane (New York: Harper and Row, 1960), p. 30.

Chapter 12

1. J. Barton Payne, *Encyclopedia of Biblical Prophecy* (New York: Harper and Row, 1973), p. 271.

Chapter 13

1. Helen Kooiman Hosier, *The Caring Jesus* (New York: Hawthorn Books, 1975), pp. xiii, 20.

2. The early church historian Eusebius said that Matthew wrote his Gospel in Aramaic. See Eberhard Arnold, *The Early Christians* (Grand Rapids: Baker Book House, 1979), p. 363.

164

NOTES

3. William Smith, *A Dictionary of the Bible,* ed. by F. N. and M. A. Peloubet (Nashville: Thomas Nelson, 1979), p. 76.

4. Jean Danielou and Henri Marrou, *The First Six Hundred Years,* trans. by Vincent Cronin (New York: McGraw-Hill, 1964), pp. 46–47.

5. E. P. Blair, "Simon," *The Interpreter's Dictionary of the Bible,* vol. 4 (Nashville: Abingdon Press, 1962), p. 357.

6. Jean Danielou and Henri Marrou, *The First Six Hundred Years,* p. 89.

7. Charles W. Forman, *A Faith for the Nations* (Philadelphia: Westminster Press, 1957), p. 60.